An Ode to
Four Four Two

T0307513

An Ode to
Four Four Two
Football's Simplest and Finest Formation

John McNicoll

First published by Pitch Publishing, 2021

Pitch Publishing
A2 Yeoman Gate
Yeoman Way
Worthing
Sussex
BN13 3QZ
www.pitchpublishing.co.uk
info@pitchpublishing.co.uk

© 2021, John McNicoll

A CIP catalogue record is available for this book
from the British Library.

ISBN 978 1 78531 838 2

Typesetting and origination by Pitch Publishing
Printed and bound in India by Replika Press Pvt. Ltd.

Contents

Acknowledgements

FIRSTLY I would like to thank Pitch Publishing for giving me the chance to share my thoughts on the game we all love. It has been the most interesting but surreal experience in my life.

To all the people who helped me along the way, however big or small in contribution, for that I am eternally grateful. Shout-outs go to Andy Ellis (Derby County historian), David Marples (Nottingham Forest), Wayne Barton, Dan Williamson and Steven Scragg (sounding boards), Stu Horsfield (Brazil), Luke Chadwick (Manchester United), Wally Downes (Wimbledon), @LUFCStats (Leeds United), Neville Southall (Everton), Ray Houghton (Liverpool) and Patrick Barclay for giving me the time to chat all things football. For anyone else I may have missed, thank you so much.

To my family. Mum and Dad I love you both. To Rachel, Matt, Megan and Jack; Taylor, Ronni, Owen and Freya; and of course Kayleigh, who put up with me stuck at the dining room table for the best part of a year. To Coxy, Danny Boy and Reidy. The boys. And last but not least to my teachers, who said that I wouldn't amount to anything if I didn't hand in my homework.

Introduction

THERE HAVE been many, many great moments in football, and achievements that are beyond a person's wildest dreams. When professional footballers are given their first contracts to sign, little can they imagine the paths that lie ahead of them. A huge percentage of footballers will have a nice career, but that's all it will have been.

For some, there has been a wealth of accolades, both on a team and a personal level.

This book takes a look at some of the greatest teams to have ever played the beautiful game and, as the title suggests, is an ode to 4-4-2. This tactic has been chosen and tailored by coaches and managers for the best part of 50 years. There have been many other formations but this one seems to be the yardstick by which all others are measured.

Football is played with a plethora of systems, from 4-3-3 and 4-2-3-1 to 3-5-2. Even nowadays, teams are looking to get the edge on their opponent by trying to be the next pioneer in terms of creating something new. But nothing is really sticking.

This book is not a tactical masterclass in the sense that I am going to be drawing arrows here, there and everywhere, and pretending to be a pundit in a studio. I do hope, though, that you can get a feel of what each manager was trying to get from his team. For every tweak of formation, there was a successful outcome. How is success measured? Some teams in his book will have held aloft the most glittering trophies available, and others reached their own nirvana.

Enjoy.

1

Formation

The Beginning

Formation
noun: **formation**; *plural noun:*
formations *the action of forming or process*
of being formed

WHEN BLACKHEATH Rugby Football Club decided to leave the Football Association in 1863, it would signal the beginning of the end of the courtship between rugby and football as we know it today. With the sports having been played together during the previous few decades, many who took part were now beginning to see a distinct split between those who were good at carrying the ball by hand and those who excelled by foot.

The first meeting of the Football Association took place on 26 October 1863, in the Freemasons' Tavern in central London. The FA set about streamlining the original rules drawn up for football, which had been written by students at Cambridge University in 1848. These were not universally accepted by all who played until 1877, when the FA produced the 'Laws of the Game', which are still in use today, albeit in a very different form as football has progressed.

The Cambridge rules were largely ignored by their northern counterparts, with Sheffield FC writing their own to accommodate themselves. A true reflection of the north–south divide! Sheffield FC are officially the oldest registered club side still playing the game. Despite this amazing record of longevity, they are not as illustrious as their city counterparts, Wednesday and United. While their younger siblings prosper in both the Championship and Premier League respectively, Sheffield FC have spent their entire history regionalised, playing in various non-league divisions in Yorkshire and the north. Local league titles apart, their highest accolade to date was achieved in the fruitful year of 1904, with the amateur FA Cup being proudly whisked back to Yorkshire.

When the FA engineered its new dossier of laws, it was to be constructed using a mixture of Cambridge, Sheffield and London rules. A league was formed in 1888 and as the 19th century drew to a close, rugby had completely marginalised itself away from any remains of football, resulting in the codes of rugby union and rugby league being formed. The Football League, which was to be the first run under full FA rule, was made up of 12 founder members: Accrington (not to be confused with Stanley), Aston Villa, Blackburn Rovers, Bolton Wanderers, Burnley, Derby County, Everton, Notts County, Preston

North End, Stoke (now City), West Bromwich Albion and Wolverhampton Wanderers.

As the years changed, so did the rules, and one of the most significant was the change in the offside rule. The original law from 1863 meant that no forward passes of any sort were permitted, except for kicks from behind the goal line. It stated, 'When a player has kicked the ball any one of the same side who is nearer to the opponent's goal line is out of play and may not touch the ball himself, nor in any way whatever prevent any other player from doing so until the ball has been played, but no player is out of play when the ball is kicked from behind the goal line.'

With football developing in the 1860s and then organically growing into the 1870s, the offside law proved to be the biggest argument between the clubs. Sheffield got rid of the 'kick-throughs' by amending their laws so that one member of the defending side was required between a forward player and the opponents' goal.

The compromise rule, which was written into the Laws of the Game in 1866, and eventually adopted universally, was an amalgamation of a form of the Cambridge rule but with 'at least three' rather than 'more than three' opponents.

Newcastle United had just been held to their sixth 0-0 draw of the season and with attendances and interest sinking faster than the *Titanic*, the FA decided to act. The offside rule was revisited and in 1925 a vote was cast and they decided that moving forward, only two opposing players would be needed between the attackers and the goal. Did the move work? Prior to the change 4,700 goals were scored in 1,848 Football League games in 1924/25.

This number rose to 6,373 goals (from the same number of games) in 1925/26. Job done by the FA.

Meanwhile, as the English leagues were becoming well established, the seeds of plantation were coming into blossom on foreign soil. As the 19th century rolled into the 20th, English folk were showcasing football to the world. The trade deals that saw pockets of English communities begin to spring up on several different continents were embroiled in not only exchanging foods and textiles but also the knowledge and workings of our wonderful game.

The early styles of play could only really be described as organised chaos. Formations, if used at all, were loosely assembled in such a way that teams were heavily occupied in the opposition half. *Inverting The Pyramid*, written by Jonathan Wilson, documents on how teams would often line up in a 2-3-5 system. This would be the benchmark until the 1920s, when managers began to improvise in order to obtain a successful result. Herbert Chapman, most notably of Arsenal and Huddersfield Town, remarked, 'No attempt was made to organise victory. The most that I remember was the occasional chat between, say two men playing on the same wing.'

Chapman built his teams around a solid defensive unit and a lightning-fast counter-attacking game. A third defender was added to his back line, something unheard of at the time, leading to a 3-4-3 formation. Back-to-back league titles with Huddersfield Town prompted Arsenal to coax Chapman down to London to showcase his craft at Highbury. More silverware followed as both the league and FA Cup were added to his growing list of honours.

Unfortunately for Chapman and Arsenal, after falling ill on returning from a scouting trip, he never recovered and died in 1934 aged just 55. His Arsenal side had dominated domestically during his spell as manager and a pioneer on these shores had been taken far too soon.

As war in Europe was brought to an end in 1945, football, although sporadically, had attempted to keep the status quo. Austrian coach Karl Rappan, who was managing in Switzerland during the mid-to-late '30s, had experimented with Chapman's formation even further. A fourth defender was added, although in a sweeper fashion, as opposed to the flat back four that we know nowadays. Rappan had paved the way for what was soon to be known as *Catenaccio* – Italian for door bolt. This enabled his teams to build from a strong defensive base, something the Italians would become famous for as the century drew on.

Another four-defender coach emerged in the 1950s. Boris Arkadiev had managed various Moscow sides including Dynamo and Lokomotiv, culminating in taking the USSR national job. Arkadiev was instrumental in how the coaching landscape would change post-World War Two. His book, *Tactics of Football*, was widely used as a go-to for most coaches worth their salt across Europe, a bible as such. His back four would resemble more of a modern-day unit, unlike Rappan's original sweeper style. The system used two full-backs either side of the two centre-backs to create a wall along the edge of the 18-yard box. The footballing equivalent of the Iron Curtain.

The Eastern bloc would prove to be a breeding ground for coaches and their new ideology of how the game should be played. Fellow Russian Viktor Maslov mirrored Arkadiev and managed several Moscow clubs during and after the war. Maslov's most successful stints were at Torpedo Moscow and Dynamo Kiev, but it was to be his invention, or interpretation if you will, of the 4-4-2 formation, that would enshrine Maslov in the echelons of the coaching world. With teams now beginning to play a fourth defender, mainly in a 4-2-4, Maslov set about creating a tactic where his two outside-forwards/wingers would track back alongside the central midfielders once possession had been lost. The idea of this was that it would become much more difficult for the opponent to break down his team with potentially eight men goal side of the ball. Once possession had been won back, the two wide players would then attempt to get as high up the pitch as possible to join the forwards.

When quizzed about his new approach to the game by a willing reporter, Maslov replied with a quote which was to define him. He likened his team and style to aviation. 'Football is like an aeroplane,' said Maslov. 'As velocities increase, so does air resistance, and so you have to make the head more streamlined.'

This was also the birthplace of the pressing game, synonymous in today's football. Pep Guardiola at Barcelona, Bayern Munich and Manchester City, and Jurgen Klopp with Borussia Dortmund and Liverpool have both followed in the footsteps of Maslov by drilling their teams in attempting to win the ball back before the opponent has the opportunity to build an attack. Rinus Michels, the Dutchman who managed Ajax, Barcelona and Holland, built his teams around the pressing game and coupled that with what he named 'Total Football'. Michels would soon become one of the most respected coaches on the planet. Johan Cruyff would play for and later model his coaching philosophies on Michels.

Viktor Maslov's 4-4-2 system and 'in your face' style was to be the foundation on which all coaches would build, similar to how Boris Arkadiev had begun a surge of new ideas after his book had been plagiarised by coaches all over the world.

The post-war 1950s turned into the swinging '60s and 4-4-2 would begin to gather momentum. England were given the honour of hosting the eighth World Cup finals, bringing the best countries in the world to London and beyond. All matches were played during the month of July 1966, taking in eight different football stadia. Old Trafford, Goodison Park, Hillsborough, Roker Park, Ayresome Park, Villa Park, White City Stadium and Wembley were to provide the backdrop on which the entertainment would play out.

Alf Ramsey, the England manager heading into the tournament, had adopted a 4-1-3-2 formation. This was to be known as the 'wingless wonders'. It was another concept of the 4-4-2 that had been established a decade earlier. The footballing fraternity would perceive England and their players to be rigid in their on-field roles. Little did they know that Ramsey would make slight adjustments to ensure that all opposition were left guessing. Instead of playing his midfield four spread out across the width of the pitch, Ramsey tucked them in to create a central overload. Bobby Charlton explained after a victory against Spain in a warm-up clash for the 1966 World Cup, 'The Spanish full-backs were just looking at each other while we were going in droves through the middle.'

Ramsey would tinker with both his system and personnel as the games came thick and fast. England dispatched Mexico and France in their group after an opening-day draw with Uruguay. The 0-0 stalemate was followed by the campaign kick-starting into life and Ramsey's men topped the group with two 2-0 victories.

A sterner test would await England in the quarter-final, prompting Ramsey to revert to his 'wingless wonders'. A slim 1-0 victory against Argentina meant that England faced Portugal in the semi-final. The game against the Argentinians would prove to be one of the most physical that Ramsey had seen unfold in front of his eyes. 'It seemed a pity so much Argentinian talent is wasted. Our best football will come against the right type of opposition – a team who come to play football, and not act as animals,' he said afterwards. England marched on. The home nation would spur England on once more in the semi-final and when the referee signalled for full time, the Three Lions had roared into the final by defeating Portugal 2-1.

The performance and style of victory in the final itself was a symbol of how just tweaking a system so subtly, can have such a wonderful outcome. England had ended the tournament as champions and were kings of the world having beaten West Germany 4-2 after extra time.

Ramsey had taken the system created by Viktor Maslov and used his own bit of magic on it. That, and a superb hat-trick by Geoff Hurst, of course.

The world stood up and took notice. Particularly in England, where coaches would begin to adopt the 4-4-2 system and try and find ways to make it even better. It would become the staple diet of every coach, manager and team across the land. Every now and again, coaches would try to be what they thought was 'innovative' by adding an extra midfielder here or another attacker there, but ultimately it was the formation which would shape the next half-century of English football.

While domestically, 4-4-2 was to take off like Neil Armstrong heading to the moon, coaches abroad were beginning to find new ways to exploit the system. Rinus Michels, and later his protege, Johan Cruyff, would employ a midfield 'pivot' in front of the back four. This would look and play like a midfield sweeper, with the extra man outnumbering the opponents' two. Sacrificing a forward enabled Michels's teams to dominate the ball in the centre of the pitch. The problem faced by coaches on these shores was that they were becoming institutionalised in their systems, and would always maintain two centre-forwards. Meanwhile, foreign teams were beginning to utilise the lone striker. Cruyff said, 'You use a knife and fork to eat. It was like that 100 years ago and it will be like that in another 100 years. The same applies to football. First the basics have to be in place, only then can the changes be made.'

As the evolution continued post-1966, so did the entertainment value of the game. With television coverage becoming more prominent, fans were now able to see their teams in action when beforehand it might have been a little more difficult for the non-attendees. English football had changed dramatically since the turn of the 20th century, as had the game on foreign soil. Despite many other coaches and particularly Michels and his philosophy, 4-4-2 was alive and kicking in a big way.

The idea was epitomised during the spoof football film *Mike Bassett: England Manager*, in which after trying to compete with the continentals and failing miserably, England manager Bassett reverted back to the tried-and-trusted system that had been ingrained into the players growing up in this country.

Football as we know it, lived it and breathed it, was about to be played by some truly remarkable sides.

2

Atlético Madrid
Simeone and the Double Block

Double
adjective: **double**
consisting of two equal, identical, or
similar parts or things

PATROLLING HIS Anfield technical area and kicking every single ball, Diego Simeone barked out orders to his team. Dressed in his trademark black shirt and matching tie, El Cholo demands the highest of standards from his players, week in, week out. Sitting on a slender 1-0 lead from the home leg in the Champions League last 16, Atlético were faced with a daunting trip to the reigning holders Liverpool. Domestically the Reds had swept aside everyone before them, bar the one and only blip away at Watford.

'Beware the Atlético Madrid sucker punch,' read *The Guardian*. 'Liverpool knew it was a possibility, however much they controlled this Champions League tie, however much they dominated in terms of possession and chances. While the margins remained slim, it could happen.'

Liverpool under Jurgen Klopp were a well-oiled machine. Their Champions League success in 2019 was soon followed by international glory the following December when they won the World Club Cup. Many had tipped the Reds to continue their great form and overcome Atléti's slim first-leg lead but unfortunately for the holders, Simeone and his men hadn't received the memo. An extra-time smash-and-grab, after a promising start from the home side, enabled Atlético Madrid to progress to the quarter-final stage.

'It was always going to take something out of the ordinary to end Liverpool's reign as European champions,' wrote *The Times*. 'It was going to require something extra special. It took this canny, crafty, infuriating but magnificently resolute team of Diego Simeone's to knock Liverpool out.'

Phil McNulty, chief football writer for the BBC, reported, 'Atlético Madrid arrived at Anfield with the usual reminders of how the stadium's atmosphere had broken the nerve and resilience of even the elite teams in the Champions League – as Barcelona found out in last season's semi-finals. Diego Simeone and his players are made of sterner stuff than that. They may have been under pressure for much of this game but not once did they buckle as they faced up to Liverpool's intensity and came out on top. Atlético simply love defending, each goal conceded almost a personal insult to Simeone – who seemed to relish Anfield's atmosphere

– and his players. After Llorente scored Atlético's second, even Liverpool looked like a side who knew there was no way they would score two goals in such limited time to progress. The La Liga side's approach may not be a thing of beauty but they are a brilliantly drilled team and this was another landmark triumph for the master coach Simeone.'

Simeone's Atléti team had become compact and hard-working. His managerial style mirrored that of his playing career in that he was tenacious, talented and carried with him a never-say-die attitude. Arda Turan, the Turkish midfielder who was at the club when Simeone arrived, was quoted as saying, 'Simeone taught us to enjoy suffering.' Simeone's players love working for him. You can tell this by the way that they work when out of possession, covering every blade of grass to try and recover the ball or break their proverbial necks to get back into the system's double block.

For the layman, the double block in football is normally considered to be when a midfield four and a back four create two parallel lines. The wide midfielders will normally tuck in to shut down any gaps through the centre of the pitch. Although not as expansive as playing with traditional wingers, the wide midfielder's role is to support in attack when necessary but more to help his team-mates plug holes and break up any passing lines when the ball has been lost. Simeone and his Atléti side had become the absolute masters of this. Effective, yes. Pretty? Absolutely not.

Appointed in December 2011 after a failed six-month stint by his predecessor Gregorio Manzano, Simeone was brought in to wrestle back some hope for the fans he had once entertained as a player. Defeat to third-tier Albacete in the Copa del Rey was the final straw for the board and they sacked Manzano. Simeone had spent the previous five seasons coaching in his native Argentina but hadn't ventured to Europe since hanging up his boots. Atléti were to become his sixth managerial role, although the Vicente Calderon Stadium would feel more like home having played nearly 150 times for the club over two spells.

The short but not so sweet reign of Manzano would soon be forgotten as the 2006 Argentinian Manager of the Year, an honour Simeone achieved at Racing Club in his first season, had set the wheels in motion and began to forge a togetherness in the squad, backroom staff, club, fans and anyone else associated with the younger of the Madrid outfits. With Atlético sitting just four points above the La Liga relegation zone, Simeone set about building a team spirit that would not only ensure that his team would avoid an unlikely relegation from the top division but at the same time also manage to embark on a successful Europa League campaign.

Atlético Madrid's top brass had seen a raft of managers and coaches through the revolving door, also known as the boardroom, since the club's last title success. The 1995/96 double-winning season under Radomir Antic, which coincidentally was Simeone's first season there as a player, saw Atlético claim both the La Liga title and the Copa del Rey. Unfortunately for the boys in red and white, that was about as good as it would get with the next 15 seasons to become a rollercoaster of both emotions and fortunes. No fewer than 18 managerial changes were to occur between

Simeone holding aloft the La Liga trophy as a player and then a scarf to the press as a manager.

Antic had managed Atlético on three separate occasions. His first foray bore the fruit of silverware in the shape of a league and cup double while his second was not so exciting. Arrigo Sacchi was given a chance to showcase his Italian flair but the decorated coach was outed by matchday 22 in 1998/99, after a five-game winless run. Antic replaced the former Milan boss, looking to revive the team's fortunes, and guided Atlético to a final standing of 13th – which was exactly where they had been when he returned.

The board decided that Antic would not be the man to lead Atléti into another new campaign and plumped for another Italian, this time in the shape of the tinker-man, Claudio Ranieri. The Valencia boss had just masterminded a Copa del Rey triumph so with his stock at a high he was shipped in on the crest of a wave. Surfers trying to find the perfect time to paddle on their board and then ride the barrel until it eventually breaks on the shore is the perfect metaphor for Ranieri's time at Atléti. Matchday 26, just four more than his compatriot Sacchi, was to prove to be the break crashing to the shore and he was replaced by Antic, back for a third spell.

By then Atlético were in big trouble. Heavy spending in an attempt to bridge the gap at the top resulted in mismanagement across the club and with debts spiralling out of control, Atléti found themselves relegated in May 2000.

Jack Porter from *The Sportsman* wrote, 'Just nine Spanish football clubs can proclaim to be La Liga champions in the competition's 90-year history. In the 1999/2000 season, a third of them were relegated from the top tier. In the very same season that Deportivo La Coruña won their first and only La Liga title in their 113-year existence, Atlético Madrid were relegated to the Segunda División alongside Sevilla (20th) and Real Betis (18th); all three former champions. A brilliantly crazy way to end the century, it remains the last time neither Barcelona nor Real Madrid picked up any domestic silverware in a single season. It also marked the first time since the early 1930s, pre-Spanish Civil War, that Atlético Madrid wouldn't be playing in La Liga.

'Atléti won just nine games for their campaign under two different managers; Claudio Ranieri, and Radomir Antić. Incredibly, they also finished runners-up in the Copa del Rey, losing out to Valencia. By that time Antić – who also predated Ranieri – was out again, replaced by former 'B' coach Fernando Zambrano, who himself lasted just under six months. Ahead of the season, Ranieri had purchased striker Jimmy Floyd Hasselbaink from Leeds United for £12m. Signed on 4 August 1999, he had been the top scorer at Elland Road for the past two seasons but Leeds refused to give him the pay rise he wanted. Though Hasselbaink would suffer the ignominy of relegation with Los Rojiblancos in his first and only season, the Dutchman did finish in an impressive second for the Pichichi in Spain, behind Racing Santander's Salva, with a haul of 24 goals.'

Antic, of Yugoslavian descent, and Italy's Sacchi and Ranieri, had broken the stranglehold of Spanish coaches at the capital club. The subsequent years were to become pretty barren. While Real Madrid were challenging in every competition they entered, Atlético were crashing from one bad season to the next. Ironically it would be the two non-Spaniards that were to steer the club inadvertently into the Segunda Division.

Atlético Madrid eventually climbed back into the top division in 2001/02, under the stewardship of Luis Aragonés, another in charge for a third time at Atlético. Aragonés had ensured that their stay in the second tier would be a short if not embarrassing fall from grace.

Things moved on and although a return to the top flight was achieved, the trophy ribbons were kept firmly in a box gathering dust. When Quique Sanchez Flores took over in 2009, things looked to be heading back in the right direction. But a Europa League success followed by a UEFA Super Cup triumph would prove to be a false dawn for the coach who would eventually make his way to English shores to manage Watford. European football was more fruitful for Flores's Atléti side as his domestic record heralded a lowly ninth-place finish in 2009/10 and a marginal improvement to seventh the following season. No one can ever take away the importance of winning silverware, regardless of priority. The problem for any Atlético Madrid manager is that just across the city is a club that year after year seems to be spraying champagne at the business end of the season.

With Flores moved on and Manzano's short stay having been and gone, it was time for Simeone to push on. 'Atlético Madrid have completed the hiring of Diego Simeone as the new coach of the Atlético first team,' read a statement on the club's official website.

'The Argentinian coach has accepted the offer made to him by the club on Thursday [to take charge] for the remainder of the season and another season, and will arrive in the Spanish capital to begin work at the helm next Monday.'

The winter break provided an ideal situation for Simeone, with a chance to create a mini pre-season training schedule on the club's return from their festive rest. Atléti were languishing in tenth and looking to be heading towards another season of mediocrity. Not to be deterred, Simeone worked tirelessly behind the scenes to ensure that every detail was examined. Minutes on the pitch, entries into the final third, goals per shot ratios and various other statistics would be scrutinised and fed back to his eager squad.

The team was littered with quality. Up-and-coming goalkeeper Thibaut Courtois had the luxury of playing behind the central defensive partnership of Miranda and Diego Godin. The South American duo, from Brazil and Uruguay respectively, completed a back line which included Juanfran and Filipe Luis. Gabi and Arda Turan were the midfield enforcers who enabled the more creative sparks to shine. The spearhead of this particular unit was the Colombian, Radamel Falcao. Prior to suffering a serious knee injury, Falcao was one of the top marksmen in the world. His backup was an emerging Diego Costa, meaning Simeone had plenty to work with.

A fifth-place finish was not to be sniffed at and with the team beginning to gel under the guidance of El Cholo, a march to the final of the Europa League would prove to be the icing on the cake of that first season. Facing fellow Spaniards Athletic Bilbao, Atlético and Simeone in particular were hoping for a cherry to add to that dessert and to take the trophy back to the Spanish capital. The boys in red and white certainly didn't disappoint as two first-half goals by Falcao blew Marcelo Bielsa's Basque side out of the water. A resounding 3-0 victory resulted in Simeone adding his name to the ever-growing list of successful Atléti managers, as Flores had done just two seasons previously. The Europa League once again showed that Atléti were the top team of the rest – those who were considered to be in the next tier below the Champions League.

Jonathon Wilson, reporting at the final for *The Guardian*, wrote, 'Marcelo Bielsa paced, he squatted, he sat down, he shouted, he looked on pensively, but whatever he did his Athletic side rarely threatened to make an impression on an Atlético Madrid team coached by one of his former players, Diego Simeone. Whatever Athletic have brought to the Europa League this season – which is a lot – however much the neutral might have wanted another of their displays of relentless attacking, tonight they were well-beaten.

'Two first-half goals from the Colombian forward Radamel Falcao won the game, allowing Atlético to spend the final hour or so sitting deep, coiled always for a breakaway. Just as important was the job done by Gabi and Mario Suárez, sitting deep in midfield and protecting the back four, preventing Athletic from ever achieving the fluency of which they are capable.'

Simeone's team had won the match despite having had only 41 per cent possession. It was the sign of things to come under the stewardship of the wily Argentinian. In the book *Origins of Possession: Owning and Sharing by Development*, Philippe Rochat wrote, 'Human ball-playing like soccer is all about control: losing, gaining, transferring and regaining control.' In a game of fetch, it is the dog who holds the majority of the possession, yet it is the master who controls the game.

Riding the crest of a wave after recent European success, Atlético headed into the 2012/13 season in confident mood ahead of a UEFA Super Cup meeting with Champions League holders Chelsea, at the Stade Louis II stadium in Monaco. Many fancied the west London outfit to nick the win but Simeone's Atléti side were victorious. Switching from their 4-2-3-1 formation that the team had used in 2011/12, Simeone brought in a more stubborn-looking 4-4-2, with Koke sitting in the hole just behind the prolific Falcao. It was to pay dividends immediately. A first-half hat-trick from Falcao was too much for Chelsea and a 4-1 win was enough to make the world sit up and take note.

The La Liga campaign was one of a bittersweet nature in that the sweetness included a third-place finish, the club's highest position for 11 seasons, but the bitter pill to swallow was that Atlético were still some way off chasing down both their city rivals Real Madrid, and the boys from Barcelona. All four meetings of that season between the clubs ended in defeat for Los Rojiblancos. A nine-point difference between Atlético and Real meant that despite a strong season against the rest, there was still plenty of work to be done to bridge the chasm at the top. Barcelona had romped to the title and held a 24-point advantage over Simeone's men.

Another sweet moment arrived at end of the season with the two Madrid clubs facing off in the Copa del Rey Final. At the home of their arch rivals, Atlético were playing catch-up from the 14th minute when Cristiano Ronaldo notched to put the favourites in front. Diego Costa equalised just before the break and the game ebbed and flowed into extra time, when Miranda grabbed the winner to send their fans wild in celebration as they clinched a tenth Copa del Rey title. *La Décima* had been achieved. This proved to both Simeone and his squad that they weren't as far away from their rivals as the league table suggested. They were playing catch-up, but with trophies coming in both his first two seasons as manager, the signs of improvement were clear to all to see.

Radamel Falcao and Diego Costa had forged a deadly partnership. Leading a two-pronged attack in Simeone's 4-4-2 system, the pair accumulated a total of 54 goals between them. For Falcao though, this would prove to be his swansong with Atlético who accepted a club record fee of £60m from Monaco, meaning the ground where Falcao had been so devastating at the beginning of the season against Chelsea would now be his footballing home.

As with all clubs, when one player leaves it opens the door for another. The Atlético fans must have been wondering why Simeone was allowing their talismanic striker to move on. A season's tally of 34 goals is a lot to replace in any standard of football, be it down the parks on a Sunday morning or in this case La Liga in Spain. The boss would show his awareness in the market though. Simeone was creating a system for his team to play, and was also collecting the players required to fit in it.

The summer of 2013 saw a real coup as David Villa of Barcelona, who had broken his leg only a couple of seasons earlier, was deemed surplus to requirements and Simeone leapt at the chance to bring in a seasoned international. A champion at club and international level, Villa himself was delighted with the chance to showcase his talents at the Vicénte Calderon. 'The signing of Villa meets all expectations,' said the club president Enrique Cerezo. 'It has been one of the signings that was most welcomed by our fans in the history of Atlético. Everyone is happy. We are delighted that Villa is with us. It is an honour.' Other notable signings that summer were the experienced Argentinian centre-back Martin Demichelis, as well as another young defender from Ajax, Toby Alderweireld.

Having defeated Real Madrid in the Copa del Rey, Simeone had the bit between his teeth, quite literally. The boss told his players, 'You have to play the games with a knife between your teeth on the pitch.' And they did just that in 2013/14. The duopoly of Real Madrid and Barcelona was smashed to pieces during the league campaign as Simeone guided Los Rojiblancos to their first title in nearly 20 years. Going undefeated in visits to both the Bernabéu and Nou Camp indicated that the tables had been turned on their rivals, with the final key result coming in a 1-1 draw on the last day of the season. Atlético just needed to avoid defeat in the Catalonian capital. Barcelona had a much better goal difference and a victory would ensure that the title would remain in the hands of Messi and co. But a Simeone masterclass ensued and a well-fought point gave Atléti the La Liga trophy to take back to Madrid.

'Atlético Madrid have done it,' wrote *The Guardian*. 'A year after they went to the Santiago Bernabéu and took the Copa del Rey from Real Madrid, they came here and took the league title from FC Barcelona. It is their first in 18 years. Next they travel to Lisbon to play their first European Cup final for 40 years. What Diego Simeone and his side have achieved is barely believable. Barcelona's supporters recognised the magnitude of what they had witnessed: when the final whistle went here, they immediately broke into applause.

'Spain suffered a collective coronary as the season headed into the final minutes of the final day with a single moment sufficient to change the destiny of the title. Barcelona's goalkeeper, José Pinto, was even up for a corner that almost dropped his way. But in the end Diego Godín's header from a corner was enough to clinch a 1-1 draw that means that for the first time in a decade Spain has a champion that is not Real Madrid or Barcelona.'

Marching into Lisbon for the Champions League Final, Atlético were buoyant. They faced their city rivals again, this time for the trophy considered the greatest in the European game. Simeone was on the brink of a historic double but was to be denied by a 93rd-minute equaliser from Sergio Ramos. Los Rojiblancos were deflated and sensing blood, Ronaldo, Gareth Bale and Marcelo completed the scoring to wrap up a 4-1 win. Simeone's side also finished as runners-up in the Copa del Rey and the Supercopa de España.

New signing Villa had chipped in with an impressive 15 goals. His partnership with Diego Costa proved nearly as fruitful as Costa's with Falcao as the pair scored an impressive 51 goal in all competitions. Having secured the title, Simeone set about making significant changes to his dressing room. No fewer than 19 players headed out of the Vicénte Calderon door, including Villa himself. The Spaniard had been offered a lucrative deal in the States with New York City and decided to see out his playing days in the MLS. Other notable exits included Diego Costa and Thibaut Courtois, both Chelsea-bound. Courtois had been on loan with Atléti for the previous three seasons but his performances were clearly being noticed by his parent club and he was recalled. Arrivals included Jan Oblak, Mario Mandzukic and Antoine Griezmann, while Fernando Torres later returned in January 2015.

With the title holders there to be shot at, the different pressures were beginning to tell on the squad and Simeone. Fighting your way to the top is difficult but it is said that once there, the most difficult part is remaining, as Atlético were soon to find out. After a huge overhaul of the squad and playing with the burden of champions, Los Rojiblancos settled for a third-place finish. Now that might seem disappointing compared to the previous 12 months but put in the context of the last 20 years, this was another step in the right direction. Only a UEFA Super Cup win over Real, a measure of revenge for the Champions

League defeat, would add any gloss to an otherwise slightly underachieving showing.

The following three seasons would show Simeone's selfish side as his defence was the meanest in Spain for those campaigns. Only 18, 27 and 22 goals respectively were conceded by a defensive unit that was so disciplined, none of the players featured in the top ten lists for fouls against or cards received. It was a truly masterful coaching lesson in that by being compact and using the double block, you don't need to tackle players to regain possession. Just cut off their supply line and watch them commit their own mistakes.

Another Champions League final came against Real Madrid in 2016. Atlético were looking to go one better than the previous final in 2014 but it wasn't to be. The final went into extra time at 1-1 and with neither team able to break the deadlock, a penalty shoot-out was required. A miss from the unlucky Juanfran meant that lightning had struck twice for Simeone and another defeat to his city rivals was tough to take for the Argentinian.

Having finished third again, Simeone once more took to the challenge of breaking the El Clasico hold in Spain. But they found themselves finishing third in 2016/17 for a third successive season and were also beaten again by Real Madrid in the Champions League, this time in the semi-finals. A year later they moved up to second and also claimed the Europa League as a Griezmann-inspired 3-0 victory over Marseille in the final continued the fine work by Simeone and his squad.

Atlético again came close in the 2018/19 campaign, missing out on the title to a Messi-inspired Barcelona but finishing above city rivals Madrid. The UEFA Super Cup was also added to the ever-growing list of honours with a resounding 4-2 victory over Real Madrid, who were now considered an ordinary side following the departure of Cristiano Ronaldo. Had Ronaldo and Lionel Messi not both been playing in the same era as this Atlético side then there would likely have been plenty more league titles for Simeone and his charges. Unfortunately for the manager and Atlético that superhuman pair haunted him for nearly a decade. Even so, the trophies won by Atlético during this period will live long in the memories of the fans. Simeone's record to date is impressive. His win rate of about 60 per cent is nearly unheard of for a top-flight manager.

'I want to thank the mothers of these players because they gave birth to them with balls this big [gestures as if holding a football],' said Simeone after a 3-1 victory over Chelsea in the 2014 Champions League semi-final. Don't ever change, Diego.

3

Derby County and Nottingham Forest
The Brian Clough Trophy

Trophy
*noun: **trophy**; plural noun: **trophies***
a cup or other decorative object awarded as
a prize for a victory or success

ONE OF the earliest signs of the 4-4-2 revolution prior to 1966 started in the lower leagues of English football. A young coach by the name of Brian Clough had taken up the vacant manager's post at Hartlepool United (still known then as Hartlepools United). Clough was forced into plying his trade as a coach much earlier than anticipated after a horrific knee injury had robbed him of his twilight playing years. His opening role was to help out with the Sunderland youth team until Hartlepools offered Clough the gig in 1965. 'I don't fancy the place,' said Clough, but he took the job anyway.

With the team from Clough's native north-east spending years precariously hanging around the deepest depths of the old Fourth Division, it was hardly a hotbed of either managerial or coaching talent. Despite the lack of glamour, the bright young manager embarked on a journey that would herald both fame and success. Assisted by his right-hand man Peter Taylor, Clough knew exactly how he wanted football and in particular his teams to play. He was stubborn in that respect and there would be no compromise. 'A team blossoms only when it has the ball,' Clough once said. 'Flowers need the rain – it's a vital ingredient. Common sense tells you that the main ingredient in football is the ball itself.'

Taylor had played with Clough, then a young striker, during their time together at Middlesbrough. Taylor had encouraged the forward to keep plugging away after initially struggling to break into the first team at Ayresome Park. But plug away Clough did, and his record of 197 goals in 213 appearances for Boro was not to be sniffed at. But despite being one of the highest league scorers in English football, Clough's managerial career cemented his place in the hall of fame. Steering Hartlepools away from the bottom of the table and finishing in a respectable top-half position, despite a minimal budget and playing staff, meant that it wouldn't be long before the reputation of Clough became common knowledge.

On Monday, 15 May 1967, the *Birmingham Post* printed, 'Brian Clough, the 31-year-old Hartlepools United manager, was yesterday appointed manager of Derby County. He will take up the post at the end of the month and is likely to be offered a three-year contract. Peter Taylor, his assistant manager at Hartlepools, has accepted a similar post at Derby. Clough's contract does not end until October, but Hartlepools are expected to release him. Taylor is free to move immediately. Derby chairman Sam Longson said, "We are very happy to have obtained Mr Clough in view of the offers he has been receiving from other clubs. We have been impressed with the enthusiasm and confidence he has shown at Hartlepools.'"

Derby had finished in 17th position prior to the arrival of Clough and Taylor. Reviewing a squad that had clearly not moved Derby towards a return to top-flight football, Clough would oversee an exodus of players over the next two seasons, culminating in a new-look team that would fit into Clough's style of play. The 4-4-2 system was now very prominent and wingers who would stay wide, spread the pitch, and get 'chalk on their boots' were now as fashionable as the turtlenecks and pencil skirts found spotted in London's West End.

Roy McFarland, the 19-year-old centre-back signed from Tranmere Rovers for £25,000, was one of the first players through the Baseball Ground door under Clough and Taylor. Liverpool had been interested but Clough and Derby landed their man. However, it seemed that not everyone was as happy about the move. The *Liverpool Echo*'s headline read 'The McFarland transfer protest' with one angry punter writing in to the local paper to proclaim, 'Sir – how depressed and discouraged must the long-suffering supporters of Tranmere Rovers feel this morning. Many of us felt that manager Dave Russell was over-optimistic in his forecast that the existing team would be good enough for the Third Division. But to release the one man to show outstanding talent (Roy McFarland) seems folly. The fee of £25,000 must gladden the directors, but what about the loyal spectators?'

Derby fans would be forgiven for believing that Clough and Taylor were just another soon-to-be-casualty added to the ever-growing list of failures in their attempt at gaining promotion. An 18th-place finish, one place lower than on their arrival, meant that there was clearly more work to be done. 'The first season was not that clever,' Clough said in his autobiography of the same name. 'Transitional, I suppose you could call it. When I first breezed into the Baseball Ground I had declared publicly that we would finish in a higher position than Derby had done in the previous season under Tim Ward. First clanger! We finished 18th. One place lower than Tim Ward, and he had been sacked!

'The foundations had been laid though; we had virtually a new side. It was improved further by the arrival of Willie Carlin from Sheffield United. Taylor and I believed in balance as well as talent and Carlin, a belligerent, aggressive little Scouser, gave us just what we needed in midfield. The picture was almost complete.

'If there was a single moment of inspiration that transformed Derby from a humdrum, dilapidated, down-in-the-dumps club, it was when Taylor took me to one side, scanned the young names in the team like McFarland, John Robson, O'Hare and Hector, and said, in an extremely serious tone of voice, "We must get some experience in this side. Go and try and sign [Dave] Mackay."'

Anyone associated with Derby might not have been so optimistic, with the club having extended their sabbatical from the top flight to 14 years, but the men in the thick of the action were slowly beginning to accumulate a group of players that could be shaped into something special. Adding Dave Mackay into the mix was only going to cement further the promotion credentials of their new-look team. The problem for Clough, however, was that Mackay was looking for a return to his first club, Heart of Midlothian. The 33-year-old, who during eight years at Tottenham Hotspur had won the First Division, FA Cup and European Cup Winners' Cup, was now looking at a return to his homeland and a swansong with his first love. 'I was a Hearts fan all my life,' said Mackay. 'I used to walk the three miles to Tynecastle, go early to get under the turnstile because I couldn't afford to get in. So when Hearts came along to sign me, I couldn't believe it. For as long as I can remember all I wanted in my life, nothing else, was to play for Hearts, which is my dream team. And to play for Scotland. I had no ambition for anything else; always Hearts.'

Clough and Taylor had other ideas. The story of the signing of Mackay is one of myth and legend, depending on who is telling it. With Mackay seemingly heading out of the White Hart Lane exit door and heading back north of the border, a determined Clough had managed to convince the Scot to head to the Midlands instead. Waiting all day in the lobby area of the stadium, Clough sat patiently, counting every second on the oversized clock above reception, until Mackay had finished his final training session with Spurs and then made his way towards the waiting manager.

In his autobiography, Clough had stated that Mackay 'looked ten years older than me' despite the player being born only a few months before his suitor. Clough took up the story in his autobiography, '"I've come to have a word with you about joining Derby." "There's no chance," he said. "I'm going back to Hearts tomorrow, to be the assistant manager, that's it."' "Tell you what, go and get in a nice bath and then we'll have a chat. You never know your luck."' Luck was clearly with Clough and Derby as an offer of £5,000 was accepted and the deal was done.

Speaking to *FourFourTwo* magazine years later, Mackay gave his version of events to a fan who had written in, asking him, 'Is it true that you were the one to ask for a transfer from Spurs? How did you feel when Brian Clough came along and signed you, calling you the "greatest ever Spurs player" in the process?'

Mackay replied, 'Because I'd had the [leg] breaks, I wasn't the same player. Brian fancied me as a captain more than as a player. It was about leadership in the dressing room. I was amazed when he asked. I was going to Hearts. After the '67 [FA] Cup Final I went to Bill Nick [Spurs boss Bill Nicholson] saying I didn't think I could do the job anymore. Hearts were going to make me player-manager.

'That weekend while I was up in Edinburgh, Brian phoned Isobel asking for a contact number for me but wouldn't say who he was so she didn't tell him. When I got back thinking we were going back up to Scotland, there, at Tottenham on Monday, was Brian waiting. By lunchtime I'd signed! You see, I'd left Hearts as a hero so didn't really want to go back older and less good; I knew I wouldn't be the same player again. I wanted to stay a Hearts hero, being a fan.'

With the ageing left-half signed, Taylor convinced Clough that the experience and know-how of the Scot would be beneficial to helping the development of the younger players and Roy McFarland in particular. Mackay would be placed alongside the bright young prospect at the heart of the defence, deployed in a sweeper role. His legs might not have been able to get him around the pitch but his footballing brain and sheer will to win would more than compensate for that. The younger players were there to provide the lungs.

Derby's 1968/69 season was a complete turnaround in comparison to the previous campaign. Having secured the marquee signing of the decorated Mackay, the wheels were put in motion on the Rams' progression out of the Second Division and back into the top flight. Having flattered to deceive in their first season, Clough and Taylor worked tirelessly to combine a team of players with the quality and slickness that was required by the manager. Taylor was the eyes, always looking for players who would fit the mould of the system, whereas Clough would be the thinking power and motivator.

Squads were small in those days, not like the numbers of 40 to 50 that you see now. Most sides were made up with the same 11 and a few reserves as line-ups were rarely changed then, especially winning ones. Derby were no different.

Andy Ellis, Derby County club historian, said that the team nearly picked itself. He explained, 'Les Green in goal. [Ron] Webster, McFarland, Mackay, [John] Robson manning the defence. [Alan] Durban, [Willie] Carlin, [John] McGovern, [Alan] Hinton patrolling the midfield, with [John] O'Hare and [Kevin] Hector up front. O'Hare was the target man with Hector being the fast forward, knocking in anything within the penalty area. Carlin was a small, box-to-box terrier, the ball-winner. Hinton, a winger and dead-ball specialist. Durban and McGovern providing the midfield skill and the attacking late runs into the box. They didn't vary the style very much and just overwhelmed the opposition midfield. Hinton created lots of goals and not many were conceded with Mackay using his experience to tell the young McFarland and Robson where to go.'

The managerial team worked in tandem beautifully, although the start to that season, and in particular the August, brought fears of another year of discontent from the supporters. Three draws and two defeats in the opening five matches doused the flames that were burning in the hearts of all Rams fans. Only when Carlin was signed in late August did the team seem to click into place and the players came alive. One defeat in the next 19 league games rocketed Derby towards the top of the pile, and during that period they kept ten clean sheets. Mackay clearly showed his presence in a team looking to be inspired by greatness. The wins kept coming, much to the joy of the ever-growing crowds at the Baseball Ground. With gates now averaging around the 26,000 mark, the town had come alive with the thought of their team heading back towards the First Division.

'Today, centre-half Roy McFarland, already an England under-23 international, left-back John Robson, right-winger Jimmy Walker and forwards John O'Hare, Kevin Hector and Alan Hinton are the personality boys who set the crowd roaring,' Peter Morris reported in *Charles Buchan's Football Monthly*. 'Not forgetting the old Spurs warhorse, Dave Mackay, no less, who for the modest outlay of £4,000 last summer could well skipper the Rams to promotion. Certainly, he has inspired their youngsters as he was meant to.

'This is no casual soccer partnership. Clough and Taylor, both ex-Middlesbrough players, long ago palled up in the Ayresome Park dressing room. 'This is what they have got, with Peter Taylor content to be the Murphy to Clough's Busby. This dedicated team job was forged when the pair were together at humble Hartlepools, learning the job the hard way. When Brian Clough was appointed manager of Derby in June 1967, he took Peter Taylor with him to share the task of restoring the great days to a club which had known scant success since their first FA Cup triumph in 1946.

'"Last April, Derby finished fifth from the bottom of the Second Division, a position which did not reflect their footballing skills," says Clough. "We were in a false position and we had some false results. But we were not ready to go up. We scored 71 goals but gave away 78 – which speaks for itself! And last season we had to meet and overcome all our troubles as well. In fact, we crammed three seasons' work into one in 1967/68."

'Clough knows the ins and outs of what is needed in First Division football. "We must be skilful – we intend to go up on skill, craft and physical stamina."'

With the champagne corks popping at the Baseball Ground in May 1969, Derby and Clough were celebrating as the team had reached the top table of English football once again. The biggest challenge was to ensure that Derby would not end up like one of the perennial 'yo-yo' clubs and slide back into Second Division oblivion. There was no need to worry as a solid fourth-place finish at the first attempt ensured that not only did the team stave off any sort of relegation fear that may have hung around Derbyshire during the summer months, but also qualified for the UEFA Cup. Unfortunately for Derby, financial irregularities and administrative errors would deny the Rams the chance to take up their merited entrance on the continent.

Unfortunately Dave Mackay's legs, no matter how youthful his compatriots around him were, could not go on forever. Colin Todd was signed to be his replacement, costing a British record transfer fee for a defender of £175,000. When Todd had been linked in the press, Clough famously remarked, 'We're not signing Colin Todd, we can't afford him.' He then did the deal that same day. Clough sent the chairman Sam Longson a telegram informing him of the signing and also the fee. Mackay headed off to Swindon but would make a return three years later as manager.

The other major signing, again chosen to fit this well-oiled machine, was Scotland's star midfielder Archie Gemmill. Clough's 4-4-2 system was now a case of picking players who would fit the puzzle as opposed to trying to shoehorn his stars in.

Winning in football can become a nice habit and if you ask any former pros, they will tell you that when things are going well anything you try will more than likely come off. Struggle at the bottom of the table, however, and you can be certain that if you lose a tenner in the morning you will probably find five pence in the evening. The habit of winning was a fine one for those players from Clough and Taylor's arrival to the crowning glory in May 1972 with Derby lifting the First Division championship for the first time.

'There were not a lot of personnel changes,' said the club historian Ellis. 'Todd for Mackay and Gemmill for Carlin, but we played the same style. Not as flamboyant as the 1974/75 championship team led by Dave Mackay, but functional (as the Arsenal team of the '90s).'

A winning mentality coupled with a fluid system heralded two titles in four seasons for Derby. After the first title, Derby flirted with success in the European Cup by reaching the semi-final before losing to Juventus in controversial circumstances. The defeat caused Clough to allege that the Italians had cheated.

Boardroom unrest and fallings out with chairman Sam Longson led to Clough and Taylor resigning from their posts only a year later. Mackay took over and according to Ellis, he continued in the same vein as his predecessor. 'Dave Mackay's [title-winning] team three years later were better, more entertaining. The 1971/72 team had been together since '68, so everyone knew their place, the system etc., and Hinton with his ability to cross the ball from either wing had some goalkeepers beaten before a ball was kicked. They could play in different ways – O'Hare was always an outlet if they wanted to get the ball forward quickly and the Gemmill/McGovern combination was pivotal. Gemmill ran everywhere with pace and McGovern is underrated (but not by Clough who took him everywhere).'

* * *

Keeping up with the Joneses is the kind of behaviour you would expect in suburban living. Mr Smith goes out and buys a top-of-the-range car to park snuggly on the drive of his newly built three-bedroom house. His neighbour Mr Graham, who has also recently moved into the street, looks out of the window of his own new house and realises that his car is in much need of an upgrade. Off to the show room he heads. He is wooed into putting down a deposit on a brand-new ride, and signs his life away to a finance deal which would put the Sopranos out of business. Look how shiny my new car is now, Mr Smith!

This is the footballing equivalent. In 1975 and with the club floundering in the Second Division, Nottingham Forest decided to bring in Brian Clough. Seeing how successful he was down the A52, the Trees were clearly hoping that lightning would strike twice back in Robin Hood country. The old adage of 'if it's not broken then don't try to fix it' could not have been any clearer in the approach taken by the successful duo. Forest, whose league standing mirrored that of the Derby team that the pair inherited in 1967, were looking for a little bit of that loving feeling. A sprinkle of the Clough and Taylor stardust that would brighten up the City Ground and end the four-season exodus from the First Division.

Clough, however, would have to wait a little longer to be reunited with his trusty assistant as Taylor was occupied down at the Goldstone Ground in Brighton until the summer of 1976. Forest had achieved a ninth-place finish during Clough's first full season with, as Taylor once wrote, a team made up mostly of 'Third Division players'.

Sometimes, as the saying goes, it's better the devil you know. With Clough and Taylor knowing exactly the system and style that they required, it was again time to find and slot together the pieces in the big Nottingham Forest jigsaw. They wasted no time in trying to bring in a few recognisable faces. 'Derby County full-back Ron Webster, is considering joining his former manager Brian Clough, at Nottingham Forest, on a month's loan,' wrote the *Birmingham Post*. 'Derby manager Dave Mackay gave Clough permission to approach Webster after a weekend telephone conversation and the player has been left to make the final decision. He will let Forest know his decision later this week.'

Although Webster eventually declined to join Forest, Clough and Taylor did opt for some of their trusted former Baseball Ground men. John McGovern and John O'Hare had followed Clough for his ill-fated 44 days at Leeds United and then moved to Nottingham from the Yorkshire club; Archie Gemmill would join them at the City Ground in 1977. With a mixture of new additions and a raft of solid players already on the books, Clough and Taylor's knowhow was certainly going to be invaluable to a team who were desperate to head back to the big time.

With the team clicking into gear and the successful partnership back in the dugout, Forest achieved their target of promotion in 1977 by finishing third in the days before the play-offs. Taylor had also begun waving his magic wand around the team. First he moved John Robertson from the middle of midfield to the left wing and then he turned Tony Woodcock into a 40-odd cap England international from a bang average reserve player. Forest had gained promotion with only 52 points, the lowest of any promotion team in history, back when it was still only two points for a win.

A record fee of £325,000 was paid out for Stoke City goalkeeper Peter Shilton, and Forest's defence would certainly be key to their success in the upcoming seasons. The return to the First Division would not be as daunting to Clough, who had led Derby to fourth in 1970 in his first top-flight season. This time around, and to the annoyance of those down the road at the Baseball Ground, Forest marched their way to the summit of the division and stayed there.

To date, Forest are still the last team to be promoted to the top division and be crowned champions of England a year later. And not only did Forest claim the title, but a League Cup Final victory over Liverpool also meant that Clough had once again turned a team from second-tier mediocrity into the finest in the land. Only 24 goals were conceded in 42 matches played with a solid defence the foundation for the attackers to rely on. Forest's regular side featured Shilton in goal, Viv Anderson and Colin Barrett as the full-backs, Kenny Burns partnering Larry Lloyd at the heart of the defence, Martin O'Neill, Gemmill, McGovern and Robertson in midfield, and a forward line of Woodcock and Peter Withe.

David Marples, who wrote the book *The History Boys*, a history of Nottingham Forest's greatest goals, reflected, 'How long have you got to explain the genius that was Brian Clough?! Numerous books have been written but if you speak to any player of that era, they all repeat the same mantra: simplicity. Everyone was crystal clear as to what their role in the team was: the full-backs' job was to stop the cross. The central defenders' job was to head the ball away from goal and stop the forward from turning. McGovern's job was to win the ball and give it to Robertson. O'Neill's job was to run up and down the wing to be on the end of a cross from Robertson and to fill in for Anderson when he went forward. Whoever played next to McGovern was to make sure he got forward if a striker went wide – and to give the ball to Robertson. The strikers were repeatedly told to hold the ball and turn to face the opposition goal.

'What is often overlooked is how good some of these players were in their own right and shouldn't just be remembered as part of a Brian Clough team. Viv Anderson, Kenny Burns, Archie Gemmill, Tony Woodcock, Trevor Francis and above all, John Robertson were supremely gifted footballers in their own right. Peter Shilton was arguably the world's best goalkeeper in this period and beyond. Other players like John McGovern, Garry Birtles and Martin O'Neill enjoyed their finest days under Clough and arguably struggled to make a similar impact elsewhere. Either way, Clough and Taylor were unparalleled in this period in their ability to build a team in which all the component parts worked, blending big signings (Shilton and Francis) with what they already had (Bowyer, Anderson, Robertson, Woodcock, Birtles, O'Neill).'

Not just happy with breaking the record fee for a keeper, Clough would also hit another transfer high by bringing in Trevor Francis for £1m in 1979. This was to be a breakthrough in the English game with no player having breached the seven-figure barrier before. Reports at the time were that Forest had actually paid a pound less, just to avoid attracting such attention, but these were never really confirmed and the fee stood. Francis would become a pivotal member of the team with his goals and all-round play helping Forest to one of the most successful periods in their history.

Like Derby, Clough never wanted to meddle with his starting 11 once they were on a roll. With squads still small and tight knit, players were hitting 30 to 40 appearances every season. His team, utilising the 4-4-2 formation, were functional and clinical with it. The core of the side after that 1978 First Division championship rarely changed: Shilton, Anderson, Burns, Lloyd, Frank Clark, O'Neill, Gemmill, McGovern, Robertson, Woodcock and Birtles.

Francis was made to work for his early starts under Clough, who kept his record signing on his toes after the groundbreaking transfer. 'Brian Clough and those who played for him were famously dismissive of tactics and notoriously never spoke of or worried about how the opposition would play,' said Marples. 'While this is true, that doesn't necessarily mean that the team did not have a plan or style of play.

'Like most teams of the era, it was a 4-4-2. However, it has been said that it was a rather lopsided 4-4-2 in that on the left Robertson was always positioned higher up the pitch – partly owing to his attacking threat and partly to his reluctance to track back. On the other side, O'Neill was tasked with, in his own words, "doggy runs" meaning he must run up and down the wing to get on the end of crosses and to help out his right-back.

'John McGovern was performing the supposed Claude Makelele role way before anyone felt that the holding midfielder required a sexier name.

'The full-backs are arguably most interesting in terms of style of play. A feature of the team would be the sight of Viv Anderson marauding down the right wing and posing a real attacking threat (hence O'Neill's role to be more diligent defensively). Likewise, the left-back (Frank Clark, Colin Barrett or Frank Gray) would not be restricted to a defensive role, even with the mercurial Robertson ahead of them. It was Barrett who slammed in the crucial goal from close range against Liverpool in the first round of the European Cup in 1978. Clark – notoriously goal-shy – found himself the furthest man forward away against AEK Athens at one stage and duly assisted a goal for Birtles. Both Gray and Anderson ran with the ball from deep through the middle of the pitch deep into opposition territory in the European Cup Final against Hamburg in 1980. They could both do this since McGovern would simply slot in defence as and when required. The utilisation of attacking full-backs was not invented by Pep Guardiola.

'Not only was this an attacking team with pace in Woodcock and Francis up front, it had attacking full-backs and John Robertson. Opposition teams were so afraid of him that they would double up against him, thus creating space for, say O'Neill, to exploit on the other side. And even when they did double up, Robertson would more often than not deliver a cross anyway – exhibit A being the 1979 European Cup Final where he evaded two Malmo defenders and delivered the cross which Trevor Francis headed in. He could also cut in from the left and use his right foot just as well as his left – exhibit B being his winning goal against Hamburg in the 1980 European Cup Final.'

With all of Clough's hard work coming to fruition and culminating in his side reaching their first European Cup final in 1979, it was clear that his team were now reaching their peak. Despite not quite managing to retain their title in the First Division, another League Cup final victory while finishing second in the table meant that a successful campaign had been enjoyed. The European Cup run, although a possible distraction, had ensured that the final was just the cherry on the cake. Record signing Francis, glancing in at the back post from Robertson's cross, saw to it that Clough and Forest would head back to Nottingham as heroes after beating Swedish side Malmo. The million-pound man looked an absolute steal as one by one the players held aloft the biggest trophy in European competition.

Forest would go on to retain their European crown the following year, this time the majestic Robertson slotting in the only goal of the game to see off Kevin Keegan's Hamburg. A Super Cup triumph was also added to the City

Ground trophy room although a hat-trick of League Cups were to be a little out of reach as Forest were turned over in the final by the less-fancied Wolverhampton Wanderers. The league campaign would see the lowest final standing since promotion as Forest finished fourth, although that did little to dampen the mood after they had again triumphed in Europe.

Marples's conclusion of this Forest team under Clough was, 'Of course, the team was capable of blowing teams away 4-0 or 5-0 but it was just as adept at hanging on to a lead once they got in front. This was arguably their strength and the great Liverpool team of this era had real problems moving them around and breaking them down.'

Clough had turned two teams into not only the best in the country, but also on the continental stage too. His use of the 4-4-2 system, coupled with roles and responsibilities of the players he brought in, heralded unbridled success. I asked Marples if the Derby–Forest rivalry had always existed, or if it had been brought on by the success of Forest once Clough had departed.

He said, 'Given the close geographical proximity between the two yet inhabiting different counties, the rivalry has always been keenly contested. Yet for all the differences (cultural as much as anything: Forest generally position themselves as cultured, big-city sophisticates while Derby push the honest, simple and genuine folk brand), they have so much in common and it is indeed Brian Clough that binds them.

'Both unreservedly love Brian Clough, and both enjoyed the best of him. Arguably, poor relations between the fans peaked in a third round FA Cup tie in January 1983 at the Baseball Ground. They didn't like each other much before and they certainly didn't after this. The subplots are almost too numerous to mention.

'Derby were on the decline and managed by Peter Taylor who had said he was retiring but then rocked up at the Baseball Ground. Taylor had Archie Gemmill in his side who had fallen out with Clough spectacularly after he was left out of the 1979 European Cup Final. Just for good measure, Gary Mills, who had played for Forest in the 1980 final, was also in the starting line-up for Derby. For Forest, Colin Todd (once a Derby stalwart) was dropped and John Robertson was four months away from joining Taylor at Derby and in doing so, precipitating the total collapse of the friendship between Clough and Taylor.

'And it was the FA Cup – the one trophy Brian had yet to win. Gemmill played a blinder and scored the first goal in a 2-0 win for his team. Forest were rubbish. At full time, Derby fans streamed on to the pitch and violence hung menacingly in the air. Meanwhile, behind the scenes, it was also very nasty. Clough tore into his defender Willie Young and accused him of throwing the game and refused to acknowledge his old mate Taylor. It's fair to say that relations between the two clubs and fans have not recovered.

'It does seem to have got nastier in the last ten years or so. The reasons for this are numerous: both are essentially very similar clubs in stature, size and history. Both are frustratingly marooned in the Championship with periods of trying to spend their way out, with disastrous consequences. And then there is Billy Davies, whose antagonistic behaviour in games between the two clubs added rocket fuel to the rivalry. I dare say that there were one or two Forest fans secretly rooting for Nigel Clough when – as manager of Derby – he kicked Davies in the leg by the touchline during a fracas. My own theory is that Nigel couldn't stand what Davies was doing to the reputation of his and his old man's club.

'Unsavoury (the word doesn't really begin to adequately describe) chants from both sets of supporters to each other about Nigel Doughty [Forest's former chairman, who died in 2012] and Mick Philpott [Derby man who was convicted in 2013 of causing the deaths of six of his children by arson] give an indication as to the depths the rivalry reached a few years ago. Some incendiary games between the two in the past ten years (red cards and pitch invasions are a given) are the stuff of legend.'

The Brian Clough Trophy was introduced in 2007 and is played for every time the two teams meet. At the time of writing, Forest hold the trophy although it is Derby, on 11 wins to their rivals' eight, who lead the way.

4

Arsenal
Boring, Boring to Invincible

Boring
adjective: not interesting; tedious

THE EMIRATES Stadium is a grand venue, situated in north London. Until Tottenham decided to upstage their rivals and build a bigger home in 2019, Arsenal had the bragging rights for the largest stadium in the capital, Wembley excluded. Their plush, 60,000 all-seater pad built in 2006 eclipsed the old ground Highbury by nearly 23,000 lovely, spacious seats, but it was the twilight years at their old home that will be remembered most fondly by Gunners fans.

Arsenal had achieved a decent amount of success during the early part of the 20th century. Herbert Chapman, who had led the team to two league titles and an FA Cup, had also pioneered the more defensive side to the game, which would be synonymous with Arsenal later under George

Graham. Chapman's Arsenal had become known as the 'Bank of England' club, partly due to its middle-class standing among football supporters, but mainly down to the fact that the attendances were so high around the 1920s and early '30s. Unfortunately for Arsenal, World War Two ripped through both their team and stadium. Despite earning success in the early '50s, the club were still reeling from having to rebuild the North Bank stand and find some new recruits. The coffers were well and truly beginning to run dry.

Bertie Mee took the Gunners to a new level and in 1971 guided his side to a domestic double of the First Division title and FA Cup. Arsenal would become a nearly club during the 1970s as five FA Cup finals would only result in one visit to the twin towers being victorious. Mind you, what a win that was! The 1979 victory over Manchester United was to be named the 'five-minute final'. Arsenal had led 2-0 until United rallied late on to score two goals in the last five minutes to send the game towards extra time, only for an 89th-minute winner from Alan Sunderland to break United's hearts and gift the Gunners the trophy.

Arsenal's century was beginning to form a pattern. Success in short spells was generally followed by a decade of barren football. It wasn't until the appointment of ex-player George Graham that Arsenal would really become a consistent household name. Mid-table mediocrity had set in at the club and Wembley appearances aside, the bread and butter of the league was a long way out of reach. The *Reading Evening Post* ran the headline 'GRAHAM IS NEW ARSENAL BOSS' in May 1986. David Wright wrote, 'George Graham, a member of Arsenal's double-winning side in 1971, was today appointed manager of the London club. Graham, manager of Second Division Millwall, succeeds Don Howe, who resigned at the end of March. Graham, nicknamed "Stroller" during his playing days, was a popular figure with Arsenal fans. He made 219 appearances for them between 1966 and 1972, scoring 60 goals. He then had spells with Manchester United, Portsmouth and Crystal Palace before hanging up his boots in 1977. The elegant midfield player was a coach at Palace before being appointed manager of Millwall in 1982. Graham said, "I am absolutely delighted to be back. When I started my managerial career, my ambition was always to manage one of the top clubs. Arsenal are not just a top club, they are THE club."'

The Scot had taken over a team which had previously finished in seventh place, and a first season at Highbury for Graham would see the Gunners show some signs of improvement. Draws instead of wins would curtail his league campaign and although they ended up in a respectable fourth spot, minor surgery was needed. While the title might have been well out of arm's reach, cup competitions were proof that on the team's day, they could compete with anyone. A League Cup final win over Liverpool, thanks to two goals from fan-favourite Charlie Nicholas, meant that a trophy to take back to north London signalled an upturn in fortunes.

Despite there being ten draws during the 1986/87 season, the defensive work had already begun on the training pitch at London Colney. Graham liked his team to be compact when not in possession. His back four had to be within touching distance of each other, to block off any gaps in between themselves. This was the era of a 42-game season and Arsenal only conceded 35 goals in 1986/87. For a midfield player, Graham certainly liked to ensure that his defence would lay the foundation on which his team would play as it is nearly impossible to build a house on just sand. An old quote, the origin of which I am unsure, says that strikers win you games but defences win you titles.

Graham, with his scalpel at the ready, begun an operation on his Arsenal side and 1987 would see the attacking prowess of Alan Smith from Leicester City and Paul Merson from the club's youth ranks brought in to help turn some of those draws into wins. Nigel Winterburn was also added from capital neighbours Wimbledon, becoming the first cog in one of the most finely tuned defences in the history of world football.

Another League Cup final was reached, and this time Arsenal were beaten 3-2 by a stubborn Luton Town side. In a game that was not too dissimilar to the 'five-minute final' of 1979, a flurry of activity inside the last ten minutes resulted in Arsenal having their hearts broken this time around. They had led the Hatters 2-1 before Winterburn saw his penalty saved and an inspired Luton levelled then went one better with a winner in the final minute of normal time.

Arsenal flattered to deceive in the league, and a sixth-place finish was not exactly where they wanted to be. The positive, again, was that for the second season running, the defence had conceded less than a goal a game. Only 39 times was the back line breached in 1987/88. Even more proof, if Graham needed it, that his side would be able to build a title charge as long as his forwards began to find the net on a more regular basis. Alan Smith topped their charts with 16 goals and even though some were vital on the road to Wembley, they were not potent enough on a consistent level in the league to worry any of the top positions.

Captain Tony Adams was the beating heart of the defensive unit, as the orchestrator and organiser of his troops. In the summer of 1988, Graham added Steve Bould to his back line signed from Stoke City. The move seemed to be a revelation for the unit as another season passed with the Gunners conceding less than a goal a game, as on only 36 occasions did John Lukic have to pick the ball out of his net. Bould's former Stoke team-mate Lee Dixon was signed in January 1989 to provide even more of a safety net.

With things behind Smith seemingly safe and sound, the striker turned it on and broke the 20-goal barrier with an impressive haul of 25. More significantly though, Arsenal had managed to not only challenge for the title, but take it right down to the wire, and to the final game of the season.

Arsenal headed to Anfield needing to win by two clear goals to win the First Division title. Liverpool needed to avoid defeat to be crowned champions themselves. 'At around nine o'clock on the morning of Friday 26 May 1989, the Arsenal players began gathering at their London Colney training ground, just off junction 22 of the M25 in the monotonous flatlands of this part of Hertfordshire,' reported Jason Cowley from *The Guardian*.

'Liverpool are to kick off, attacking the Anfield Road End. The first chance of the match falls to Arsenal, when Bould arrives from deep to head a cross towards goal; the ball beats Grobbelaar, only to be headed up and over the bar by a retreating defender.

'Liverpool start the second half by seeking to dictate play. During the break, The Kop are chanting, "Champions, champions." Smith has found space and he's there, alone, with his marker distracted by Adams, about six yards out; with the lightest of touches he glances the ball into the far right-hand corner of the net, with Grobbelaar beaten before he has had the chance even to dive.

'"I was just trying to get the team to concentrate, to concentrate hard, and then we'd have another double," McMahon says. "Even today people come up to me and mention that one-minute-to-go moment. I try to laugh it off, but it still hurts.'

'From the touchline Theo Foley is screaming at Lukic, urging him to release it. For fuck's sake hit it, fucking hit it. "I was calling him every name under the son," Foley says. "I couldn't believe he wanted to throw it out to Dixon."

'Smith receives the pass and, with his usual unostentatious economy of movement, turns to play the ball through to Thomas, rushing forward from midfield.

'Sensing danger, Grobbelaar moves towards Thomas just as he reaches the edge of the penalty box. Thomas, free, must feel the hot rush and strain of their exertion. He has the ball and is moving towards the penalty spot. The goalkeeper is coming towards him. Thomas has the ball. He is waiting for the goalkeeper to commit, just waiting; it

AN ODE TO FOUR FOUR TWO

goes up and over the goalkeeper and continues on its way into the net. 2-0.'

Despite Graham shocking Liverpool, and even his own players for that matter, Arsenal were institutionalised in their 4-4-2 style. The players were only told on the day of the Liverpool encounter that they would be playing with a sweeper, as to not cause them too much panic. On this occasion the switch worked beautifully.

'It's harder to stay on top than it is to make the climb,' is a quote by the legendary women's basketball coach, Pat Summitt. The American was an Olympic medallist and coached over 1,000 wins at college level, before being inducted into the Women's Hall of Fame in 1999. The following season, Arsenal were to find this out as once again deficiencies in front of goal hampered a title defence. Smith, who had hit 25 goals in the championship-winning campaign, struggled to match the feat and plundered just the 13. The rearguard, however, playing as a compact, well-drilled unit and only conceding on average one goal per game, backed up Graham's belief that his team were still as good as anyone on their day.

Not wanting to rest on his laurels, Graham made a significant signing who turned out to be one of the most understated captures during the club's modern era. David Seaman was signed for a then record fee for a goalkeeper of £1.3m, bringing him from west London to north. Queens Park Rangers were trying to persuade John Lukic to move in the opposite direction but he saw his future back at Leeds United. The board at Highbury need not have worried about splashing so much of their hard-earned coin on a new number one. The Yorkshireman would make an immediate impact with his new-found employers, as well as the North Bank faithful, and only pick the ball out of his net on 18 occasions in 1990/91.

Dovetailing with this defensive masterclass, the Jekyll and Hyde finishing of Alan Smith ensured that the Gunners would again claim the First Division title in Seaman's debut campaign. Smith this time broke the 20-goal barrier on his way to a second medal in three seasons. 'Arsenal became the first team this century to win the championship with only one defeat,' posted the *Sunday Independent* (Dublin). 'So another league season came to a close and Arsenal can look back with pride. They hammered Coventry 6-1 at Highbury, including a hat-trick from Anders Limpar, to win the title by seven points from Liverpool.'

The team had nearly completed an invincible season, bar a single 2-1 defeat at Chelsea on 2 February 1991. No team had gone a whole season unbeaten in the modern era. Only Preston North End in 1888/89 had achieved the feat. Sport and particularly football, had moved on to a more professional standing since then.

During that season there was to be a more iconic moment, albeit for the wrong reasons. The original battle of Old Trafford in October 1990 saw the first and only time in English football that teams had been deducted points for actions on the pitch. The Gunners were already on a suspended sentence for failing to control their players in a game with Norwich City in 1989. One thing was for sure, these players representing both Graham and the club were more than willing to fight. 'Midway through the second half, fighting broke out between the players after a clash between Limpar and United full-back Denis Irwin. I remember Nigel Winterburn setting the tone by ploughing into the melee with a waist-high, scything tackle,' wrote Michael Hart, who had been present reporting for the *Evening Standard*.

'As many as three players from each team could have been sent off by referee Keith Hackett, who simply couldn't keep up with what was happening. Irwin and Brian McClair kicked out at opponents and Paul Ince dived on Limpar. Winterburn, Limpar and Paul Davis were the main skirmishers on the Arsenal side. The fighting lasted 20 seconds and 21 players were involved. Only Arsenal goalkeeper David Seaman was not.'

When Hackett finally restored order, he cautioned two players – Winterburn and Limpar. The fact that the match had been broadcast to 64 countries guaranteed a swift response from the FA. Both clubs were charged with bringing the game into disrepute and failing to control their players. Arsenal knew they would bear the brunt of any FA punishment because they had been involved in a similar incident against Norwich the previous season. Arsenal chairman Peter Hill-Wood swiftly acknowledged that what had happened at Old Trafford was unacceptable. In an unprecedented move, the board fined the manager, George Graham, and five players – Winterburn, Davis, Limpar, Rocastle and Thomas – two weeks' wages. United fined three unnamed players.

If Arsenal hoped their decisive action would forestall a points deduction by the FA, they were wrong. Urged on by UEFA, the FA summoned Hackett and officials from Arsenal and United. After three hours of deliberation they announced £50,000 fines for both clubs with Arsenal docked two points and United one.

The two title wins had coincided with Alan Smith hitting the net on a regular basis, either side of his blip in 1989/90. So going into another title defence, instead of waiting to see if it was going to be a fruitful season or not for Smith, Graham delved into the transfer market and nabbed Ian Wright from Crystal Palace in September 1991. Wright, who had broken his leg a couple of seasons previously and fired himself on to the big stage after his brace in the FA Cup Final in 1990, found himself heading to north London from Croydon to give Smith a little helping hand. Wright notched his first of 185 Arsenal goals in a League Cup debut against Leicester City. Just days later, a hat-trick on his league debut against Southampton ensured that the England forward would get off to a flyer. For me, Wright was a more iconic player than Thierry Henry of later years. Henry scored an amazing amount of goals and eventually overtook Wright's record. Henry played in an absolutely world-class side whereas Wright was coming to an Arsenal in transition yet still managed to score an audacious amount of goals each season.

The inception of the Premier League meant that there was now even more money to be divided up between football's top tier. What was once a paltry TV payment shared out among the so-called big clubs was now swatted aside for a multi-million-pound package for one and all. Arsenal, though, despite dominating the remaining few seasons in the old First Division, were toothless in the inaugural campaign of England's new top flight. A tenth-place finish was recorded and Wright managed to contribute 30 in all competitions, with 15 coming in the Premier League. His team-mates had relied so heavily on the hitman that they seemed to have forgotten how to score themselves and the Gunners would finish the season with the lowest goals scored, 40, of any team in the division.

Once again, though, Graham's team would prove to be a match for anyone on a one-game basis. Twice the Gunners flexed their muscles to overcome a stern Sheffield Wednesday side and win both domestic cups against the Owls. The FA Cup Final was decided by a replay, with Arsenal running out 2-1 victors, which had earlier been the same score in the League Cup Final. Goals from Wright and Andy Linighan, either side of a Chris Waddle strike, meant that the FA Cup was heading to Highbury and a Wembley double had been secured. Paul Merson and Steve Morrow had reversed a John Harkes strike to win the League Cup.

The mid-1990s would be synonymous with Arsenal and cup competitions as their league form seemed to be more of a mixed bag during that time. A mid-table finish in 1992/93 was masked over with qualification for the now defunct European Cup Winners' Cup, although the 1993/94 campaign would see an improved domestic effort with the Gunners finishing in a more respectable fourth spot. European adventures might have meant that the extra travel and games had an adverse effect on the players, but when it came to the continental competition they banished any fears. Arsenal marched to the final of the Cup Winners' Cup and faced a decent Parma side containing Gianfranco Zola.

Wright had once again scored over 30 goals in all competitions but this time his fiery character was about to come back and bite him as suspension ruled him out of the showpiece in Copenhagen. Graham opted for an attack of just Smith and the boss's decision was justified with the target man scoring the only goal in a tight final. The 1-0 victory would coincide with a shift in tactics and formation as Graham had opted to move away from his favoured 4-4-2 and opted for a stubborn 4-5-1. Wright, though, would have his day in the sun and a year later Arsenal again reached the final, looking to retain their title.

The 1994/95 season could be named as the 'we could have' campaign. A massively disappointing domestic season culminated in a 12th-place finish, and an early exit from the FA Cup coupled with a quarter-final defeat in the League Cup meant that it had been a pretty terrible year on British shores. But in Europe Arsenal again swatted aside all before them to reach a second European Cup Winners' Cup Final in two seasons. This time around, however, the Gunners were not to be sipping on champagne, even with the inclusion of the talisman Wright. To rub salt into the wounds, ex-Tottenham Hotspur midfielder Nayim scored an audacious goal from around 45 yards with the game seconds away from a penalty shoot-out. Real Zaragoza had taken the lead midway through the second half but John Hartson pounced to level the scores, only for the sucker punch to come right at the end. The long-range hit-and-hope from Nayim caught David Seaman completely by surprise. The stopper was quickly back-tracking but was to soon realise that there was nothing he could do to stop the ball looping over his head and into the net.

Arsenal 'could have' retained the Cup Winners' Cup, 'could have' done much better in the league, and 'could have' marched to Wembley on two different cup competitions. But they didn't. In fact, by the time they had reached the Cup Winners' Cup Final in Paris, the Gunners didn't even have the same manager in the dugout. George Graham, who had transformed the club in his time, was at the centre of a rogue transfer deal. He was let go by Arsenal and subsequently banned by the FA from football for a year.

'The Football Association yesterday published detailed findings of this summer's disciplinary commission which found the former Arsenal manager, George Graham, guilty of misconduct and suspended him from all football activity until 30 June 1996,' reported *The Independent*. 'The following are edited extracts from the commission's "Statement of Reasons":

'Uniquely, for a disciplinary hearing, the procedure involved a prosecution case, presented by Brian Leveson QC for the FA, and a defence, conducted by Anthony Arlidge QC for Graham. The charge concerned an alleged breach of Rule 26(a)(x) governing "misconduct... or any improper behaviour likely to bring the game into disrepute". It related to the transfers of Paal Lydersen from IK Start to Arsenal in November 1991 and John Jensen from Brondby to Arsenal in July 1992. The three members of the commission were: Geoff Thompson (chairman, Sheffield and Hallamshire FA), Gordon McKeag (Football League president) and John Reames (Lincoln City chairman).

'The prosecution case. Mr Leveson put the charge, in summary, in three alternative ways:

'(1) most seriously, that Mr Graham had effectively conspired (with Mr Rune Hauge, a football agent) to make a personal profit from the Lydersen and Jensen deals;

'(2) that the payments arose out of or in connection with the transfers, and he knew that was so when he received them;

'(3) that the payments were connected to the transfers, but Mr Graham did not realise this.

'It was clear from Mr Arlidge's final speech that he broadly accepted that it was helpful to look at the case on these bases. 'The chronology of events was subject to a considerable degree of agreement between the FA and Mr Graham.'

Bruce Rioch was chosen to replace Graham, but his time was to be limited and he spent just one season in the job. A fifth-place finish, only achieved on the final day, meant that Arsenal had scraped into a UEFA Cup position. Rioch's legacy, though, would be that he brought Dennis Bergkamp to Highbury. The Dutchman joined from Inter Milan for a fee of around £7.5m. It was reported by several sources that Rioch had lost the respect of some of his players and when disputes with the board rumbled on, it was inevitable that his tenure was not going to be everlasting.

Rioch was dismissed in the summer of 1996. David Dein decided that they would not rush in to a decision to replace him but instead install Pat Rice and Stewart Houston to temporary manager positions. It wouldn't be too long, however, before the man who made Arsenal a modern-day powerhouse showed up at the marble halls of Highbury.

Arsène Wenger, who was coaching in Japan, was given the job in September 1996 and quite frankly not many people had heard of him. A successful spell in charge of Monaco, with a side including Glenn Hoddle, Mark Hateley and George Weah, was on his CV. Wenger had clearly made a good impression on Hoddle, who thought that the Frenchman was well ahead of this time regarding coaching.

Hoddle recalled, 'I've got to say what Monaco did [compared] to Tottenham in those days in 1987 was so much more advanced. The first day Mark Hateley and myself went to walk off after a two-hour session and Arsène told us to go over to the fitness coach to warm down for 45 minutes. Me and Mark looked at each other and said, "What's a warm-down?" Everything was structured and organised to the second so I could tell straight away what he wanted from his individuals and from his team. There was instant clarity. I had never worked so hard; three sessions per day in the first week was [like] nothing we'd done in England. It was very, very tough training, but you got fit.'

Even with the lack of knowledge surrounding the new man at the helm, Arsenal fans had nothing to fear.

What their new boss had in store for them was a blend of attacking football infused with grit and determination. As mentioned before, it's impossible to build a house on sand. What Wenger found on his arrival was a group of defenders who were a colossus in terms of doing their respective jobs. Goalkeeper David Seaman was usually joined by full-backs Lee Dixon and Nigel Winterburn and any two from Tony Adams, Steve Bould and Martin Keown in the heart of the defence. The forward line was as menacing as any in the division as Ian Wright and Dennis Bergkamp had begun to strike up a very interesting partnership. The midfield, though, was not as strong as Wenger would have liked.

Patrick Vieira was signed from AC Milan prior to this arrival of Wenger, although it is understood that the manager was very much involved in the transfer beforehand. Vieira, Wenger's fellow Frenchman, was a very large unit of a man but was very agile at the same time. The first season under Wenger began very well with the use of tactics that were very foreign in style but British in execution. Wenger toyed with changing the traditional shape but was soon told in no uncertain terms by skipper Adams that if he was going to get the best out of his troops, then he should play to their strengths.

Hoddle saw first-hand at Monaco how tactically astute Wenger could be. 'Arsène was very positive with the way he set his teams up and got that across to me very quickly in our first meeting and that was what I was impressed with,' explained the former Spurs man.

'I remember the first pre-season game we had and he just said to me "you're coming too deep", because I used to come very deep at Tottenham on the right-hand side of the diamond formation.

'He played me behind the striker Mark Hateley and he said, "I've got two players in midfield," which was an absolutely similar system to when he first went to Arsenal. He had two holding players that could really use the ball well. That was Emmanuel Petit and Patrick Vieira at Arsenal. We had Marcel Dib and Jean-Philippe Rohr at Monaco. He said, "That's their job to defend. You defend from the front, organise, mark the wingers, but we need to get the ball to you."

'That was something that was different for me straight away but I could understand it and it suited me as a player and the team. We settled into the team pretty quickly and won the title. We were very dominant. We played some wonderful football; he loves to play creative football. He knew what he wanted from the team. It was pretty clear-minded; you had clarity when you went on to the pitch of the shape that he wanted and how he wanted us to play.'

Arsenal had led the Premier League at the tail-end of winter in 1996 but a leaked story about Wenger's private life seemed to knock the stuffing out of both the Frenchman and Arsenal. A third-place finish meant that the Gunners had just missed out on Champions League qualification, by goal difference to Kevin Keegan's Newcastle. In keeping with the French flavour, Wenger had already raided his homeland for Nicolas Anelka in February 1997 and then added Emmanuel Petit, Gilles Grimandi and Christopher Wreh the following summer. Fan favourite Paul Merson was sold to Middlesbrough and replaced by explosive Dutch winger Marc Overmars.

Wenger took his new-look squad for a pre-season trip to Austria, which was soon to become the norm for him. The boss decided to give his players a well-deserved night off as the workload presented to the team had been gruelling to say the least. Ray Parlour recalls an obvious split in the cultures as the British lads headed off to the bar while the French players would go for a coffee and a smoke. 'How are we going to win the league this year?' said Parlour. 'We're all drunk and they're all smoking.'

Arsenal began the 1997/98 season with indifferent form. A team meeting was held by the players and coaching staff in which it was reported that a few 'home truths' were dished out. It clearly had a positive effect on the squad as they regrouped and one game at a time they hunted down champions Manchester United. Ferguson had already crossed paths with Wenger after the Frenchman had bemoaned the hectic Christmas period. Fergie made quite clear his feelings on Wenger's credentials to be trying to change English football, 'He's no experience. He's come from Japan and he's now telling everybody in England how to organise their football.'

A vital 1-0 victory over United at Old Trafford in March 1998 brought a new-found belief that Arsenal were still in the title hunt. Bookmakers had begun paying out on United retaining their crown after holding an 11-point lead going into the game. Overmars scored the only goal and catapulted Arsenal along on what became a ten-game winning streak. Not only did they manage to reel in the reigning champions, they overhauled them. Wenger became the first foreign manager to win the top division in English football. And, not happy with just that, Arsenal also claimed the FA Cup with a 2-0 win over Newcastle United at Wembley to clinch the double in only Wenger's second season in charge.

The emergence of the young Nicolas Anelka meant that it would be the end of the road for Ian Wright. The forward who had wowed the North Bank for the last eight seasons was heading to east London and West Ham United. Many supporters were wondering if this was a smart move, seeing that Wright had netted a club record 185 goals in his time at Highbury. Anelka, though, was deemed the future of the team. A resounding 3-0 win over United in the Charity Shield, with Anelka scoring, suggested that Wenger and Arsenal would continue in the same vein.

Having clawed back the deficit of points the season before, it was Arsenal who stormed off into the distance in 1998/99. The campaign though was to become one of the most hard-fought in the history of the club, and Arsenal would end it with only that curtain-raiser at Wembley to show for their efforts. Manchester United clinched the title on the last day with a win over the Gunners' rivals Tottenham, after a season that had seen both teams going toe to toe, like two heavyweight boxers slugging it out in the ring. Arsenal had defeated United at Highbury but failed to capitalise on their early-season dominance.

The teams squared up again in the semi-final of the FA Cup and required a replay at Villa Park, which was heading to extra time when Phil Neville's tired tackle brought down Parlour. In the final minute of normal time, Dennis Bergkamp had the chance to book a second final in two years but a penalty save by Peter Schmeichel and wonder goal by Ryan Giggs in extra time meant that the Gunners would end the season empty-handed.

In August 1999, Wenger managed to secure a deal to bring the out-of-favour Thierry Henry from Juventus. His idea was to pair Henry with fellow Frenchman Anelka. What Wenger was not planning on, however, was an offer from Real Madrid for Anelka. Wenger knocked it back but word soon spread and reports of unrest from his player meant that with much annoyance, Wenger had to accept the deal.

United would dominate the next two campaigns, winning three titles in a row from 1999–2001. Wenger's team, though, pushed them hard on all three occasions. A 2-1 FA Cup Final defeat to Liverpool in 2001 was the last straw for Wenger, who had stuck by his team as a show of loyalty. Henry was singled out as missing chances in the final, although these comments were to be kept in house. Robert Pires and Freddie Ljungberg were signed to freshen up the squad and Sol Campbell was persuaded to join from across north London. Signing Campbell was another masterstroke from the boss, who had somehow managed to nab Tottenham's club captain.

The team was now one built on strength in positions. Wenger and his side meant business while United, who had been the best team in the land over the previous few seasons, were beginning to start a period of transition. Arsenal took full advantage of United's weakness and played some breathtaking football with the link-up play between Pires and Henry a joy to behold. Henry seemed to galvanise the team into a safety net of 'if we just do our jobs, Thierry will win us the game'. Henry was sensational. His 30-goal haul ensured that not only did the Premier League make its way back down the M1 in 2002, but also another FA Cup was added into the mix. Ray Parlour and Freddie Ljungberg were the scorers in a London derby victory over Chelsea, albeit one played many miles away in Cardiff as Wembley was beginning to be rebuilt.

Henry didn't just stop there and was really starting to enjoy himself. An indifferent beginning to life in an Arsenal shirt was soon forgotten as he began to thrive in a partnership with Bergkamp, dovetailing with Pires behind them. Arsenal in 2002/03 would retain their FA Cup with a slim victory over Southampton in the final, Pires scoring to end Saints' resistance. Unfortunately for Wenger, a David Beckham-inspired United pipped Arsenal to the Premier League title.

The 2003/04 season started like any other and there was some new blood brought in. Cesc Fabregas was signed from Barcelona and with David Seaman nearing the end of the line, Borussia Dortmund's Jens Lehmann arrived to provide more competition in goal. Four wins from the opening four games signalled the Gunners' intent, then an early-season meeting with Manchester United resulted in a 0-0 draw which turned out to be one of the most infamous games in Premier League history.

'The "Battle of Old Trafford", as it came to be known, saw two teams who genuinely hated each other spend most of the game fouling one another (overall, 31 fouls were committed by both teams) before setting off a mass brawl after the final whistle' wrote the *Daily Cannon*. 'The flashpoint was the antics of United striker Ruud van Nistelrooy, who managed to get Patrick Vieira sent off by provoking him into a second yellow card. Hence, when the Dutchman stepped up and missed a late penalty, the Arsenal players wasted little time in confronting him.

'In the aftermath, Arsenal were fined £175,000, and several players were banned. Lauren was suspended for four games, Martin Keown got three games while Vieira and Ray Parlour received one each. Meanwhile, the rather fortunate fact that van Nistelrooy, a top striker in his day, missed his penalty meant that Arsenal were still unbeaten in the league.'

The clocks changed to signal the end of British Summer Time but Arsenal's fortunes did not as wins were becoming more constant and the momentum continued. Victories over Leeds, Liverpool and Chelsea in the run-up to the festive period give Arsenal a strong platform to play from as the calendar scrolled into 2004. The Gunners were red hot after the turn of the year and won nine games on the bounce before the run was halted by a 1-1 draw at home to Manchester United.

Thierry Henry was finding the net with consummate ease as the season continued. The service he was being supplied was as slick as a Formula One pit crew but sometimes the Frenchman would just do it all on his own. In all competitions he racked up 39 goals, 30 of them coming in the Premier League. Leeds, Liverpool and Chelsea were again dispatched in the second half of the campaign and as the games began to run out, Arsenal and Wenger were looking at a season with zero in the defeats column.

A team largely made up of Jens Lehmann, Lauren, Sol Campbell, Kolo Toure, Ashley Cole, Ray Parlour or Freddie Ljungberg, Patrick Vieira, Gilberto Silva, Robert Pires, Thierry Henry and Dennis Bergkamp had swatted away all before them and on 15 May 2004, they became the 'Invincibles'. A 2-1 victory on the final day over Leicester City had immortalised those men into the fabric of the club and hearts of supporters. Important supporting roles were also performed by the likes of Sylvain Wiltord, Pascal Cygan, José Antonio Reyes and Edu.

'For a time it appeared that they were just like the rest of us mortal,' wrote Dion Fanning for the *Sunday Independent*. 'Arsenal's final step to immortality was in trouble after 45 minutes at Highbury yesterday. Paul Dickov, an ex-Arsenal player and a man who was, mainly unwittingly, part of one of the many dark stories of the season's Premier League which contrasted so bleakly with the beauty of Arsenal's football, put Leicester City ahead in the first half and Arsenal looked doomed to just a run-of-the mill Premier League trophy. They had seen the treble collapse in the space of five days in April and it appeared that the final hurdle to matching the record set by Preston in the first season of the Football League in 1889 would not be cleared.

'Arsène Wenger has relentless ambitions for this Arsenal side and the failures, particularly in Europe, would have disturbed him ever since Manchester United and Chelsea ended his great ambitions for the season. Defeat yesterday would have been a further unwelcome irritant. But Wenger is a great manager and his few quiet words at half-time put his side back on the right track and the manager can now add Arsenal to Mutzig, the team he played for in the French Third Division which went through that league unbeaten.

'In the second half, the champions arrived. Thierry Henry scored from the penalty spot and Patrick Vieira, even more important to this side than his compatriot up front, skipped into the box to score a second. Arsenal had secured their eternal reward, an achievement greater than Preston's, who played only 22 games in a nascent championship, but perhaps also an indication of the weakness in the Premier League. You cannot get a realistic price on any contender outside the top three.'

Wenger had embraced the 4-4-2 system with his iron-tight defence, hard-working midfield and explosive attack. His wingers were not as orthodox as many teams before him, but they were devastating nonetheless.

5

Brazil

The Samba Boys

Samba
noun: a Brazilian dance of African origin

BACK BEFORE the internet was invented and everything was readily available at the touch of a button, the common football fan would have to wait every four years to see the beautiful sight of Brazil at a World Cup finals. Vibrant colour and noise would follow the Samba Boys everywhere they travelled. There was always something quite romantic about seeing those bright yellow shirts on the TV. The skills and tricks that would accompany the football would mesmerise the watching world.

The 1982 Brazil side is among a small group to sit in a special yet unwanted category. The rather unfortunate title belonging to the trio is that the teams in question are considered the best to never actually win the World Cup. Hungary in 1954, Holland 20 years later and then Brazil

1982 wowed their respective competitions and competitors alike but failed to lift the world's most famous football trophy. The middle of the 20th century would see arguably one of the earliest cases of international domination. The Hungary national team, who were to also be remembered as the 'Magical Magyars', embarked on an unbeaten run from 1950 all the way through to the World Cup Final itself in 1954. You are probably thinking that they may not have actually played that often over a four-year period, other than the odd friendly or qualifier here and there, but you would be mistaken. The Magyars played 50 matches in total, which included 42 wins, seven draws and only one defeat.

The Hungarians even had the audacity to roll over England on two separate occasions. The first meeting was billed as the Match of the Century. A Ferenc Puskas-inspired team dominated England on the Wembley turf in 1953 and ran out 6-3 winners. The return match a year later in Hungary would see an even bigger margin of victory as the Magyars really were magical that night as England were sent home with their tail between their legs. Hungary took the spoils in an emphatic 7-1 dismantling of the Three Lions.

England, though, should not have felt so hard done by as thrashings by Hungary were to become as common as London buses. South Korea and West Germany were dispatched 9-0 and 8-3 respectively in the group stages of the 1954 World Cup. A quarter-final victory over the fancied Brazilians meant that Hungary's march to the final was still unhindered. That win against Brazil was to be known as the 'Battle of Berne' as both teams spent the game carrying out nothing short of assault on each other. The fighting even carried on in the tunnel after the final whistle. Nevertheless, a 4-2 scoreline extended the run.

Semi-final opponents Uruguay were to be the most resilient and extra time was required to break down the South Americans and land a place in the World Cup Final. Hungary's opponents would be their group stage compatriots West Germany. The Germans had rested quite a few first-team players for the group match against Hungary, so despite that mauling they were in confident mood. This encounter was labelled the 'Miracle of Berne'. Hungary had raced into a two-goal lead before a stubborn German side rallied and overcame the odds to win 3-2. On their 50th and most important match of their unbeaten run, the Magical Magyars had no more rabbits left to pull out of the hat.

The Dutch side of 1974 were a different animal altogether. As mentioned previously, Rinus Michels was the conductor of this beautiful orange orchestra. His Total Football philosophy heralded a new wave of football coaching. Players moved with freedom and could usually play in a variety of positions. 'It is an art in itself to compose a starting team, finding the balance between creative players and those with destructive powers, and between defence, construction and attack – never forgetting the quality of the opposition and the specific pressures of each match,' said Michels. His team included the incredibly talented double act of Johan Cruyff and Johan Neeskens.

Orange flags were spotted as far as the eye could see as the Dutch began their tournament with a 2-0 win over Uruguay. The second group game against Sweden, although ending up as a 0-0 stalemate, will be remembered for including one of the most iconic moments in footballing history. In fact, the moment was so special that the movement is now coached and used the world over. The Cruyff turn was born on this day in June 1974 as Cruyff, who was attacking but facing his own goal, rolled the ball with the inside of his foot between his own legs and turned the poor Swedish defender inside out. Holland met an Argentina side who were still waiting for the emergence of Diego Maradona, and put them to the sword in a 4-0 win. East Germany and Brazil also fell by the wayside as Michels's team, marauding through the tournament with flair and ease, made their way to the final. West Germany, again the chief protagonists to this story, were lying in wait. Neeskens got the Dutch off to a racing start with a second-minute goal before a battling Germany side again tore up the script and turned the tie around a 2-1 victory.

Now you might be wondering what this brief turn back in time has to do with the 4-4-2 formation and while I do slightly digress, it brings me to the third element of this unfortunate trio. Brazil in 1982 were considered to be a worldwide love story. Their scintillating play and attacking verve had every young footballer out on their local green pretending to be the next Zico, Socrates and Falcao.

The midfield of this side was made up in a non-conventional style, as you would expect with a Brazilian line-up. The onus was on attacking and flair, dazzling their opponents into submission. When the finals began in 1982, Brazil kicked off their campaign with a hard-fought 2-1 victory over the Soviet Union. They outclassed their opponents but made hard work of getting the result done and dusted, looking a little rusty in the process.

Stu Horsfield, author of *1982 Brazil* and content provider for *These Football Times*, wrote, 'The Brazilians lined up for the 1982 finals to a soundtrack of samba drums and rhythmic dancing cascading down from the stands of the Estadio Ramón Sánchez Pizjuán. Enthusiasts, pundits, writers and tactical experts have pondered over manager Telê Santana's formation and selections during the tournament, the most common conception being a 4-2-2-2 formation relying on the full-backs to provide width and two holding midfielders providing cover for two attacking midfielders who supported the front two. At times the almost chaotic and cavalier commitment to attacking football was presented as a 2-7-1 formation, with two centre-halves staying back, while the full-backs provided width to a midfield five, leaving just a lone striker at the top of the formation.'

With only Eder supplying any actual width, it was down to the remaining three players to control a four-man midfield. Zico, Falcao, Socrates, Cerezo, Dirceu and Isidoro were told that they would have to rotate between themselves to occupy the right-hand side. Eder would stay wide and left, trying to support the lone striker Serginho. Zico was more a number ten who would drop a little deeper than the forward lines and try to pick up balls in between defence and midfield. The system was to be two men holding in midfield with two supporting attacking players. The problem with this is that the words defence and Brazil go together like oil and water. It was dysfunctional and chaotic at best. If the Brazilians themselves didn't know what was going to happen during a game, then how on earth were their opponents meant to?

Scotland and New Zealand were the unlucky recipients of the Samba Boys' rust being dislodged. A 4-1 win over the Scots was followed up by another emphatic 4-0 victory over the Kiwis. Topping their group and heading into the second group phase, Brazil were in fine fettle. Horsfield described the play in as much beauty as the football itself, 'The Seleção's midfield was a rotating carousel operating at a carnival – it was loud and vibrant, and had the entire planet waiting and wanting to enjoy the ride.'

Bitter rivals and reigning champions Argentina lay in wait for Brazil. The two South American heavyweights, meeting for the third time in the finals, would again go toe to toe. Argentina had dispatched Brazil on their way to the 1978 crown but the boys in yellow avenged that defeat in the hot Spanish sun. Goals from Zico, Serginho and Junior ensured that there would be no repeat of the previous encounter. Argentina did manage to pull one back, but it was to be just a consolation.

The 3-1 victory over the world champions had brought a level of excitement to neutral supporters that had not been seen before. Italy were Brazil's final opponents in the group, having stumbled through the first group phase. Three draws and only a couple of goals scored had somehow been enough to ensure qualification. Cameroon were bizarrely eliminated from the competition as the Azzurri had scored one more goal – two to the Africans' one, and both teams had a goal difference of zero. This was enough though to jump-start the sluggish Italian players and prior to the Brazil victory over Argentina, Italy had tasted a triumph of their own. Argentina were beaten 2-1, meaning that their subsequent defeat to Brazil had ended their chances of retaining their title.

Telê Santana's Brazil needed just a draw to secure a semi-final berth and lead to the mesmerising cacophony of Serginho, Zico and the rest of the gang facing Poland in the last four. Italy, with their *Catenaccio* approach, had clicked into gear with their previous victory over Argentina still fresh in their minds. Despite Socrates and Falcao finding the net for the Samba Boys, a Paolo Rossi-inspired Italy were 3-2 victors as a hat-trick from Rossi ended the dreams of the 1982 edition of the Seleção.

Horsfield, writing for *These Football Times*, documented, 'Telê Santana had told his distraught players in the dressing room, "The whole world has been enchanted by you. Be aware of that." The Brazilian coach received a standing ovation from over 300 members of the press as he walked into the room for the post-match press conference, acknowledgement indeed for what Santana and his team had given to the world.

'During their five games, Brazil had scored 15 goals and seen seven different outfield players score. But it wasn't about the number of goals or the numerous sublime and artistic ways they found to put the ball in the net. It was about their philosophy, their imagination, their style, their grace, their instinct, their love of the beautiful game, all played to a pulsating samba soundtrack.

'Sadly the mesmerising quintet never played together as a unit for Brazil again. They had been brought together through circumstance and only shared a pitch for four games and 20 minutes. But the memories and emotions those five exceptional players produced will reverberate through the rest of time.'

Santana's side played possibly the most unconventional form of 4-4-2 that anyone had ever seen. Fast forward a dozen years and a more rigid version was about to become the blueprint of a World Cup success. The 4-2-2-2 that was used in a more hectic fashion in 1982 was to make way for a new, almost robotic version.

The 1994 World Cup was the first to take place on American soil and was everything you would expect it to be. Full of razzmatazz, including an opening ceremony which involved Diana Ross taking a penalty into a goal, the singer skewed her kick miles wide, with the goal exploding into two halves like she had scored a howitzer. In a tournament that saw the arrival of Russia, after the break-up of the Soviet Union, and a German side joined together for the first time since before World War Two, Brazil, managed by Carlos Alberto Parreira, were heading into the tournament as one of the favourites although unrest back in their homeland meant that they had it all to do.

Parreira was branded a dinosaur and heavily criticised for his wooden 4-4-2 approach. His build-up to the finals was poor at best. After they had been held by Graham Taylor's England and eliminated in the quarter-final of the

Copa America by rivals Argentina, the press at home were nothing short of scathing. The beautiful artistry of Zico and Socrates was replaced by methodical, workmanlike players. Captain Dunga was the recipient of the majority of the finger-pointing. The under-fire coach would give the country the Holy Grail, but just not in a way that they would want it. History proves that the best team doesn't necessarily always triumph. Ask any fan in the world if they would prefer style over substance and you would get a mixture of responses. For me, it's about holding the trophy high above your head at the finish line. How you get there is another story.

An opening match against Russia would give Parreira's men a chance to shake off their defensive tag. True to form, though, the manager selected two holding midfielders in Dunga and Mauro Silva. Both players were charged with sitting in front of the defence, acting like a shield and enabling the full-backs to get forward. This was way before Claude Makelele made the role cool. Back then it was a symbol of pragmatism and negativity. The attacking two of the four were to provide Bebeto and Romario with the ammunition in which to fire the team to success. Rai and Zinho had underperformed in the previous matches under the coach, but were still trusted to start.

It's always good to kick off any tournament with a win, especially when the media have already condemned your campaign before it's begun. Romario's goal and a penalty from Rai meant that the Samba Boys had achieved not only victory but also a clean sheet. A 2-0 win was the perfect start for Parreira.

When you gain momentum, you never want to stop. Luckily for Brazil, they only had to wait four days for the next group game. Opponents Cameroon were the surprise package four years earlier at Italia '90. The majestic Roger Milla had won the hearts of millions with his goals and corner-flag dances before quarter-final defeat to England ended the dreams of the Africans, so this would be no gimme for Parreira's side. Romario edged Brazil into a first-half lead and when Cameroon defender Rigobert Song was red carded in the 63rd minute, the task was made all the more difficult for Milla and co. Further goals were added by Marcio Santos and Bebeto in a solid 3-0 performance.

It was another clean sheet, yet still the clamour for attacking football back home was felt by both players and coach. Johan Cruyff, then Barcelona coach, wrote at the time, 'The secret of football is to keep control of the ball to pursue the goal. Only Brazil did it. For sure they could play more offensively and with more beauty, but there's moments when the spectacle has to be sacrificed.'

With two wins from two and rivals Russia, Cameroon and Sweden all dropping points in the group, qualification was done and dusted. The remaining tie against Sweden was not so much of a dead rubber as both teams were capable of topping the group, and the Swedes were no mugs. Their squad included the likes of Thomas Ravelli, Stefan Schwarz, Henrik Larsson, Roland Nilsson and Thomas Brolin. The Brazil team was left unchanged with the coach insisting that consistency and continuity would be key.

Sweden took the lead midway through the first half with Kennet Andersson breaching Brazil's back line for the first time in the campaign. Mauro Silva was hooked at half-time and Mazinho entered the fray. The move paid dividends immediately as just two minutes after the restart, Romario levelled. The rest of the match was a case of both teams settling for what they had and by the time the referee had blown for full time, neither side were beginning to break sweat. This did not go down well with the locals, who had paid good money to see two teams strolling around in the Pontiac Silverdome.

Brazil topped the group and progressed to the knockout phase where the hosts, the USA, awaited in the last 16. They had drawn with Switzerland, beaten Colombia and lost to Romania. They had posted the third-best record of the teams who finished third in their groups, allowing them to progress. The rock star-looking Alexi Lalas marshalled a five-man defence while the exciting prospect in midfield, Cobi Jones, looked to provide the upset that the home fans craved.

The home team, driven on by their partisan support, stifled Brazil. Parreira's side could only huff and puff at a well-organised Stars and Stripes defence. Mazinho had kept his place in the midfield at the expense of Rai, which ultimately meant that Brazil were playing with three traditional holding midfielders, leading to another groan from the press. Why would a team as imposing as Brazil need to start with such a midfield? The game was a poor representation of what a major finals spectacle should contain. The red card in the first half to defender Leonardo did little to help the flow of Brazil.

There are many iconic moments in football. Some have been played over and over, and what happened to win the game is definitely one of them. A routine header from a clearance had found its way towards Romario. The forward was in an offside position and was walking back towards the halfway line, clearly in no mood to join in with play, when not only did he let the ball bounce past his shoulder, his defender followed suit. Bebeto was on to it like a flash. The USA were playing an extremely high line so that they could suffocate the Brazilian midfield. With no real width in the team, the plan was working a treat until now. The speedy forward raced through on goal, coaxed the goalkeeper off of his line, rounded him and finished into an empty net. The 77th-minute goal will be remembered for what happened afterwards as Bebeto, Romario and Mazinho headed to the touchline to begin the baby rocking celebration that is well remembered today.

The *Sandwell Evening Mail* reported, 'Lalas looks more like a rock star than a soccer star, this guitar-playing American. But he gave a big-hearted performance against the Brazilians that has epitomised the American World Cup dream. True, he was partly to blame for the goal but he could not be faulted for effort and commitment, and he made some telling tackles.'

The Samba Boys had marched into the quarter-final but more abuse from the fans back home had reached the coach and the team. Parreira had no intention of either changing his playing style or his starting 11 as again Mazinho was given the nod over Rai for the clash against Holland. The Dutch side were a team in transition as the all-conquering squad of 1988 was beginning to make way for new talent. The devastatingly quick Marc Overmars, the attacking flair of Dennis Bergkamp and midfield guile of Frank Rijkaard would prove to be a stern test to a Brazil team that had been more pedestrian than explosive.

Over 60,000 fans crammed into the Cotton Bowl, Dallas, but the first half proved to be something of a non-event as both teams looked scared to death of giving away a goal. With a much needed arm around their shoulders during the half-time break, Brazil began the second period in devastating form and double act Romario and Bebeto fired goals in quick succession to open up a comfortable lead by the 63rd minute, or so they thought. A minute later, Dennis Bergkamp pulled one back to set up a grandstand last 25 minutes, then Holland nicked an equaliser and probably thought they had Brazil on the ropes until Branco scored with eight minutes remaining to claim a 3-2 win.

Brazil's opponent in the last four were their group associates Sweden. Just like the first encounter, the game was dull at best. If Brazil were the wolf to this script then Sweden were the three little pigs' brick house and had little to no intention of mounting any sort of meaningful attack. Instead it was wave after wave of blue shirts penetrating the Swedish midfield to mount attacks. Sweden held firm until a red card for Jonas Thern midway through the second half. Brazil smelt blood as the ten men still had around half an hour to try and survive in the sweltering Pasadena heat. With only ten minutes remaining, a deep cross to the far post was headed in by Romario and Brazil were through to the final.

Pasadena was the venue for the culmination of the tournament and Brazil, already familiar with the territory, were not to be fazed by the 90,000-plus crowd. Finals were nothing new for this football powerhouse, although the current crop of players were not held in such high esteem as their predecessors. Needless to say, reaching a final of any tournament should never be sniffed at. Some countries can only dream of such prestige, while for some, it's just another day at the office.

The press were not being fooled by Brazil's path to the final. The *Aberdeen Evening Express* ran with the headline 'Simply the Best'. The statement, though, was held more in regard that the two teams facing off for the trophy were part of football's royalty as Brazil v Italy was considered a clash of two footballing heavyweights. The same paper also commented, 'Brazil had a defence that has not really been tried, a midfield that with the failure of Rai, had no real spark. Thank god for the forwards.'

Carlos Parreira had described his job as 'a death sentence', although despite this he would stick to his footballing principles and philosophies. His starting 11 to face the Azzurri included goalkeeper Taffarel, and full-backs Jorginho and Branco, with Marco Santos and Aldair completing the 'untried' back line. The four-man block of two defensive midfielders and two attacking midfielders were the same unchanged quartet from previous rounds as Mauro Silva and Dunga again provided the defensive muscle with Zinho and Mazinho tasked with supplying the bullets for the tank-like Romario and nimble Bebeto.

The comparisons to the Italian side were identical as both had relied heavily on two players on their route to the final. Dino Baggio and Roberto Baggio – no relation

– were the catalysts for Italy, as much as Brazil had banked on Romario and Bebeto to plunder the goals. Both managers had become increasingly under pressure due to performances and playing style. Arrigo Sacchi had found his head framed by a gunsight on *World Cup Daily Edition*. The Italian coach also favoured a 4-4-2 formation (more on this later), albeit a slightly more traditional approach than the South Americans. Italy's line-up included the linchpin of the defensively astute AC Milan team. Captain Franco Baresi would play as a sweeper in a four with the young Paolo Maldini alongside him acting as his legs. Dino Baggio occupied the centre of the pitch while Roberto led the line.

Those hoping for a repeat of the 3-2 megamatch back in 1982 were quickly brought back to modern-day reality. Full-back Jorginho was substituted with just 21 minutes on the clock and was replaced by a young, up-and-coming defender named Cafu. Italy provided just the one meaningful attack for both sides during the first 45 minutes. Brazil were poor, but not as poor as the finishing from both Bebeto and Romario. When they needed them most, both players spurned chances at the back post when it was possibly harder to miss than score. Bebeto skewed his kick back into the arms of the hapless Pagliuca while Romario's side-footed effort found the wrong side of the post.

Extra time brought no clearer indication of who would go on to win this tie and so for the first time in the history of the World Cup, a penalty shoot-out took place to decide the overall champions. Was there ever likely to be any other outcome considering the form and styles of both teams?

Italy went first. Up stepped Baresi who fired wildly over the bar and into the packed terrace behind Taffarel's goal. Brazil, though, failed to take advantage as Marcio Santos placed his shot to the goalkeeper's right but Gianluca Pagliuca guessed correctly to palm away and ensure parity.

Demetrio Albertini and Alberico Evani both finished with confidence for Italy, but so did Romario and Branco for Brazil and the shoot-out was tied at 2-2 with the pressure becoming as intense as the red-hot Pasadena sun. Flowers need water to survive in the sunlight but Italy were about to be drained of any chance of evolution. Daniele Massaro, Baggio's strike partner, stroked a tame kick slightly to the left of Taffarel, who easily saved. This time, Brazil did not fail to capitalise.

Dunga, showing why he was trusted to take the armband, drove his spot kick to the goalkeeper's left. Pagliuca chose right and the tide had turned. It was now advantage Brazil. Roberto Baggio, the 1993 FIFA World Player of the Year, Ballon d'Or winner and World Soccer World Player of the Year, was charged with scoring to level the shoot-out. As Baresi had done, Baggio blasted his kick waywardly over the crossbar. The only thing his penalty threatened was a passing plane.

Brazil had done it and against all of the unrest back home, they had claimed an unlikely World Cup victory. Or that's what the press and fans believed. Whatever was said about Parreira and his squad, you will never take away the fact that they won the greatest prize of them all. Stylish? Sporadically, yes. His unconventional midfield quartet were more Gary Barlow than Robbie Williams. Parreira found a way to win. He used the players at his disposal and believed that the process was the correct one.

The formation had continued but the coach did not, and the 1998 World Cup finals in France presented the chance for Mário Zagallo to shine. The system was identical although there would have been a different set of roles for the players. A 4-2-2-2, similar to Parreira's, was rolled out in which an identical midfield plan of two defensive midfielders was tucked in behind two attacking midfielders. Romario was gone and replaced by Ronaldo.

Brazil would again reach the final, looking to retain their trophy. Victories over Scotland and Morocco ensured qualification despite a defeat to Norway. A 4-1 rout over Chile followed by a 3-2 win against Denmark meant that another trophy win was well in reach, although Brazil needed a penalty shoot-out victory against the Dutch in the semi-finals to meet the host nation in the showpiece in Paris.

Unfortunately for the holders, a Zinedine Zidane-inspired France rattled in three goals without reply. Controversy surrounded the final itself with the fitness of Ronaldo questioned in the build-up. Rumours were that the player was not fit but his sponsor Nike was pressuring him to play. Edmundo, who was benched, said, 'Nike's people were there 24 hours a day, as if they were members of the technical staff. It's a huge power. That's all I can say.' But of course this was all just speculation and maybe France had just been the better side. The 1998 Brazil team would be considered much more entertaining than the class of

'94. But there's a huge difference in getting over the line. Parreira's team did that.

As Dunga lifted the golden trophy high above his head in 1994, he screamed at the gathering press, 'This is for you, you treacherous bastards! What do you say now? C'mon, take the pictures, you bunch of treacherous motherfuckers! It's for you!' Clearly the pressure had told on the squad with the constant barrage of negativity. Despite this, though, back home on the streets of Rio de Janeiro, those fans partied like their ancestors had done before them. Champions of the world. Beautiful yet uninspiring. Brazil and their unconventional 4-4-2.

6

Manchester United
The Sir Alex Ferguson Era

Era
noun: a long and distinct period of history

HIS PLAYERS lined up on either side of the tunnel to form a guard of honour. Their manager was set to take to the Old Trafford pitch for one final time. Sir Alex Ferguson had announced his retirement a few days previously and this time he meant it.

Ferguson had initially planned to retire in 2001 but, fortunately for the club and Manchester United fans all over the world, he was talked out of it by his family. This time around though, it was final.

The crowning glory of that long, last walk from changing room to centre circle, was that United had clinched yet another Premier League title, taking Ferguson's haul to 13 domestic wins. The boss brought the curtain down on the 2012/13 season, and his 26-year stint at Old Trafford, by addressing the crowd. Ferguson took the microphone and said, 'I've got no script in my mind, I'm just going to ramble on and hope I get to the core of what this club is meant to be. First of all, it's a thank you to Manchester United; not just the directors, not just the medical staff, the coaching staff, the players, the supporters, it's all of you. You have been the most fantastic experience of my life. Thank you.'

He continued, 'I have been very fortunate. I have been able to manage some of the greatest players in the country, let alone Manchester United. All these players here today have represented our club in the proper way – they have won a championship in a fantastic fashion. Well done to the players. My retirement doesn't mean the end of my life with the club. I will now be able to enjoy watching them rather than suffer with them. If you think about it, those last-minute goals, the comebacks – even the defeats are all part of this great football club of ours. It has been an unbelievable experience for all of us, so thank you for that. I'd also like to remind you that when we had bad times here the club stood by me, all my staff stood by me, the players stood by me – your job now is to stand by our new manager. That is important.'

With all the fanfare and tears of Sir Alex's retirement, those of an older generation will remember the contrast in which the Scot arrived. Ron Atkinson had been relieved of his duties on 6 November 1986 having brought back an exciting brand of football to Old Trafford after the pragmatic era under Dave Sexton. But two FA Cups and a stop-start title attempt were not enough to keep Big Ron in the job after five seasons in charge. The board acted and Martin Edwards moved to bring in Ferguson from Aberdeen. Edwards said the decision had to be made 'in light of the team's poor performance over the last 12 months' and 'in the best interests of club and fans'.

Glasgow clubs Rangers and Celtic were and still are, the powerhouses in Scottish football. Ferguson took the job at Pittodrie and immediately set about trying to break the stranglehold of the two giants. He wouldn't have to wait long. In his first two years he won the Scottish Premier Division and then followed it up a couple of seasons later with a memorable European Cup Winners' Cup Final victory over Real Madrid. The Scot from Govan clearly had pedigree, which prompted Edwards into heading north for his man in November 1986.

United's lowly position of 21st in the First Division didn't deter Ferguson. He accepted straight away and set about a journey which, when talked about in years to come, will sound like the stuff of fairytales. Granted, the beginning was no smooth ride. No signings were made with Ferguson wishing to assess his squad before making any changes, and the team managed to climb to a final mid-table position of 11th.

Ferguson spent over a quarter of a century at Old Trafford, most of which was successful. In between all of the trophies and celebrations there were also times of unrest, upheaval and failure. During his tenure, Ferguson endured his fair share of criticism, with the brunt of it coming around the time of his third full season. The banner 'Three years of excuses and it's still crap... Ta-ra

Fergie' was made famous both back then and at the end of Ferguson's reign, following unbridled success.

Manchester United teams under Ferguson consisted of three cycles, with each one containing a transition period, some stabilisation, and then dominance. The manager could sense that his final season in charge was to be the starting point of the next cycle and with the years no longer being kind to him, he felt the time was right to step aside.

Cycle One

Viv Anderson was to be the boss's first signing in the summer of 1987, with Brian McClair also joining from Celtic. A year later, Mark Hughes was re-signed from Barcelona and goalkeeper Jim Leighton came in from Aberdeen. The stopper had served Ferguson well in the past and the manager was hoping for a similar impact. United, as well as going for tried and tested signings, dipped their toe in the market to bring in some young blood and a 17-year-old Lee Sharpe arrived from Torquay United.

The team had suffered the same domestic sequence under Ferguson as under Big Ron with a decent fist of a title tilt being followed by a false dawn the following year, although the league positions under Ferguson were generally a lot lower than Atkinson's. But Ferguson's first full season showed promise as a runners-up spot hoodwinked supporters into thinking that the team was nailed on for a push the following campaign. They weren't, and another 11th-place berth led to Ferguson eventually opting to bring through some youth players to mix with his squad.

The 1989/90 campaign was a bittersweet time for the Scot with another dismal showing in the First Division, the team finishing in 13th position and only five points clear of relegation. The manager had spent big as well, in the shape of club record signing Gary Pallister for £2.3m from Middlesbrough. But it didn't stop there with a further £1.5m being spent on Neil Webb from Nottingham Forest and £750,000 on Mike Phelan of Norwich. Amid all this, fan unrest was becoming increasingly regular.

Ferguson was on thin ice. It is the general consensus that Mark Robins's goal away to Nottingham Forest in the third round of the FA Cup saved the boss that season and while I agree that it was of the utmost importance, it was merely a cog in a wheel that kick-started a chain of events that unfolded over the next five months. Was it more important than Clayton Blackmore's goal against Hereford? Or the winner scored by Brian McClair away at Newcastle United in round five? Or the extra-time equaliser by Mark Hughes to secure a replay in the final itself? Without all of this, United would have no doubt suffered elimination, culminating in Ferguson losing his job.

As it happened, a Lee Martin chest and volley put paid to a spirited Crystal Palace team and brought Ferguson his first trophy at United. The 1990 FA Cup was the catalyst of the first cycle. The manager had shown that he was not afraid to make big decisions. After an erratic season Jim Leighton was dropped for Les Sealey ahead of the final replay. The Scottish custodian had suffered a terrible loss of confidence and would never be seen again in a United shirt.

The final two seasons of the old First Division would see a much greater improvement to both the style and the playing staff. A sixth-place finish in 1990/91 was a big improvement on the previous season, although defeat to Big Ron's Sheffield Wednesday in the League Cup Final had slightly skewed the progression of the team. United, though, saved their best until last and a season's finale in Rotterdam with a head-to-head against Johan Cruyff's Barcelona in the European Cup Winners' Cup Final. The competition showed that Ferguson and his United team were ready to mix with the very best and the much-fancied Barcelona were put to the sword. Two Mark Hughes goals against his former side were enough to claim a historic victory and a trophy that Ferguson had won nearly a decade before at Aberdeen was added to the previous campaign's FA Cup.

The wheels were in motion. The team's style had been a mismatch of systems but Ferguson had now started to utilise a 4-4-2 formation which played with direct wingers. Hughes was the ideal target man while Brian McClair would alternate between dropping into the hole or playing on the shoulder of the last defender. Lee Sharpe had quickly emerged as a quick, tricky winger, with an eye for goal. The 'Sharpey Shuffle' celebration was soon to be on show at stadiums all over the country, much to the annoyance at times of the boss. Russian winger Andrei Kanchelskis was signed from Shakhtar Donetsk in 1991. Kanchelskis was lightning quick and is probably the most direct winger I can ever remember see play at Old Trafford. Peter Schmeichel, a monster of a goalkeeper, was brought in and soon replaced cult hero Les Sealey. The Great Dane was another superb piece of business for a modest fee of around £500,000. Schmeichel, although largely unknown at the time, soon imposed himself on his team-mates and opposing forwards.

The beginning of the 1991/92 campaign highlighted the importance of signing a rock-solid number one as Schmeichel kept clean sheets in his first four matches, until a 1-1 draw at Old Trafford against Leeds United dented his record. United's rivals were to prove to be a Yorkshire thorn in their Lancastrian side on more than one occasion that season.

The new and exciting brand of football played by United that year would again intrigue the natives and another youngster was thrown into the mix. Ryan Giggs, a Salford lad, had flirted with some first-team appearances a year earlier. Like Sharpe, Giggs was a tricky winger who loved to get the ball at his feet and attack opposition full-backs. The winger combinations of Giggs, Sharpe and Kanchelskis were a dream for Ferguson, with both youngsters being able to operate on either flank.

United would not drop below second place for the entire season. Unfortunately for them, it was also a position they would finish no higher than as Howard Wilkinson's Leeds would catch a faltering United in the final furlong and the Red Devils choked at yet another title charge. Defeats at West Ham and Liverpool condemned Ferguson and his squad to a runners-up medal and the trend that Ron Atkinson had started was still being continued by Ferguson.

United fans could be forgiven for thinking this would be the case once again as the opening games of the 1992/93 season saw them beaten by Sheffield United and Everton.

Ferguson then bolstered his squad with the signing of Dion Dublin, who made an immediate impact in more ways than one as United beat Southampton to kick-start their campaign, Dublin scoring to send the away fans into raptures as the Red Devils held on to their 1-0 win to move to 11th.

The cheers soon turned to tears for new man Dublin as a broken leg in the fixture against Crystal Palace just 14 days later curtailed his season. 'Dion has a fractured fibula, but even more serious is the damage to his ankle ligaments,' said Ferguson. 'He is going to hospital tonight for an operation, but it looks as though he is going to be out for four to five months. It's a killer blow for us, and devastating for Dion. We'll miss him.'

Despite this, United were off and running and when Leeds came to town a week later they saw off the champions 2-0. Ferguson, however, was left with a conundrum. Dublin would be on the treatment table for the foreseeable future which again left him light in the striking department. Some things just happen for a reason. When Leeds boss Howard Wilkinson phoned to enquire about Denis Irwin, Ferguson replied that he was not for sale at any price. As quick as a flash, the Scot fired back at Wilkinson with a request of his own. How about Cantona?

There had been reports of unrest between manager and player in Leeds. Cantona, having played his part in the title win of 1992, was still not flavour of the month with his boss. Wilkinson agreed a deal could be done and in November that year arguably one of the most important transfers in the history of Manchester United was concluded. Little did anyone at the time know the impact of that chance phone call about Irwin. In later years Bryan Robson claimed he was worried about Eric's reputation for 'flitting from club to club, staying nowhere very long and generally causing trouble', while Mark Hughes said he 'wondered whether it would end in tears'.

It was a breath of fresh air for the team as the Frenchman arrived with little fanfare from across the Pennines. The transfer coincided with a run of seven wins from nine games, with no defeats during that period. United were as good for Cantona as he was for the team. The manager set up the side with the Frenchman operating in a free space just behind Hughes. Cantona's first goal arrived in December as United drew 1-1 at Chelsea and then the Frenchman embarked on a four-game goalscoring run of his own. United were beginning to pick up the pace and turned performances into points, and Cantona was pivotal as Ferguson's side began to gain momentum. Their main rivals for the title were Aston Villa, who at the time were managed by Ron Atkinson.

United were determined not to fall short again when it mattered most at the business end of the campaign, and the Easter weekend victory over Sheffield Wednesday was the turning point. Wednesday, who had taken the lead through ex-Leeds player John Sheridan, looked to tilt the championship back in the favour of Villa. As the game drew towards its climax, United looked dead and buried but a late corner was swung in and Steve Bruce's fine header looped over Chris Woods and into the far corner of the net.

Old Trafford erupted. A point had been saved, or so everyone thought. With the referee having to receive treatment during the match, there was a significant amount of stoppage time and in the 96th minute another United attack led to a Gary Pallister cross, which deflected off a Wednesday defender and looped aimlessly into the sky. Bruce, leading by example, buried the header into the far corner. The roof went off the place. Alex Ferguson and Brian Kidd were beside themselves and were dancing on the pitch. The referee eventually blew his whistle and it was advantage United in the battle for the championship.

By May, with Aston Villa needing to win at home to Oldham to keep the fight going, the pressure was now on the side from the Midlands. Atkinson's men could not find a way to win and United were handed their first top-tier title in 26 years. The season was rounded off just a few days later when United defeated Blackburn Rovers 3-1 at Old Trafford to start the coronation. Blackburn, meanwhile, had been heavily backed by local businessman Jack Walker. Alan Shearer, among others, was lured to the Lancashire town to begin what was to be a whirlwind romance of football. They finished in fourth place, just one point behind Norwich City, narrowly missing out on qualifying for European football in their first season back at the top division after promotion a year previously.

United's title win was to begin a period of almost total domination in England. Young Irishman Roy Keane had been signed to add midfield class with Bryan Robson appearing less and less in the first team. In May 1994, Captain Marvel announced his decision to become player-manager at Middlesbrough. Keane was brought in from Nottingham Forest for a British record of £3.75m and was viewed as Robson's long-term replacement. Forest, having been relegated during Brian Clough's farewell season, were reluctant to let their star man go but Ferguson got the deal done – and what a deal it turned out to be.

United cruised to another title in 1993/94, fending off Blackburn, who were beginning to look the part with their swashbuckling style of football. It was similar to what was being played out at the Theatre of Dreams, with wingers getting high and wide, whipping in crosses to centre-forwards who absolutely thrived off them. Blackburn had pushed United close but fell away when it really mattered, while Cantona had again shone. His goals and link-up work were becoming synonymous with the way in which Ferguson wanted this team to play.

Cantona did, however, find himself at the centre of flashpoints throughout the season, showing that for all of the brilliance that came with the Frenchman there was also a dark side lurking underneath. Cantona had got involved in a scuffle away in Turkey when United played Galatasaray in the Champions League. He was also sent off for a stamp on John Moncur at Swindon and was then dismissed again just days later as two bookings in a short spell at Highbury led to another early shower. But for all of the madness, there was also the sublime. On his return from suspension, Cantona hit a brace in the derby to beat Manchester City 2-0.

Having had to wait over a quarter of a century to retain the top flight trophy, United managed to claim it in two successive seasons and in 1994 they also threw the FA Cup into the mix and beat Chelsea 4-0 in the final, Cantona again netting twice. United could have claimed a domestic treble, had Aston Villa not spoiled the party by beating them 3-1 in March's League Cup Final.

The bookies, and certainly fans of United, would not have bet against them making it a hat-trick of titles in the 1994/95 campaign, especially after another good start to the season and when they beat Blackburn 1-0 at Old Trafford in early January, Cantona with the only goal, it looked inevitable that the championship race was only going to head one way. That is, until that fateful night at Selhurst Park. With United not playing particularly well, Crystal Palace defender Richard Shaw had clearly seen from opposition defenders how to get on top of the Cantona in games. In a flash, Cantona had clashed with Shaw and the forward was again heading to the changing rooms before his team-mates.

What was to follow was something that I had never seen before or since. With Cantona heading along the touchline to the corner of the pitch towards the tunnel, all seemed as normal as can possibly be when an opposition player is given his marching orders. Of course you get the odd word and shout as you head off but nothing a player hasn't heard before. Then out of nowhere, the forward lunged in a karate kick-style motion, towards a supporter on the opposite side of the advertising hoardings. Cantona, then jumping to his feet, rained some punches on the fan before being dragged away to the safety of the dressing room.

It resulted in Cantona being banned from all football until October, nearly eight months later.

Andy Cole had been signed from Newcastle United for £7m to bolster the forward line earlier in the season. Cole had been prolific at Newcastle but took a while to adapt to life at Old Trafford. United battled on in Cantona's absence but the talisman was sorely missed as Blackburn pipped United to a third title by a single point. They were beaten by Liverpool at Anfield on the final day but United were unable to unlock a stern West Ham defence at Upton Park. Had Cantona played, I'm pretty certain that there would have been a third title in three seasons. But the hurt wasn't finished there as United also went down to a stubborn Everton side in the FA Cup Final, Paul Rideout's goal the difference as again Ferguson's men were toothless in attack.

Earlier we looked at the three cycles of Sir Alex Ferguson's reign at Old Trafford. The first cycle was brought to an abrupt end during the summer of 1995 as Andrei Kanchelskis, Mark Hughes and Paul Ince were all allowed to leave, to Everton, Chelsea and Inter Milan respectively. Many around the world thought that the United manager had lost his marbles. Ferguson, however, had seen behind the scenes that there was a crop of young players coming through the ranks who were determined to put United back on top.

Cycle Two

Eric Cantona was still missing from the side but despite his absence, United boasted a host of talent, so the opening day of the 1995/96 campaign was a shock to the system. The team contained a mixture of old and young as United were dealt a body blow by Aston Villa, going down 3-1 with the youngsters seemingly out of their depth at Premier League level. Criticism was being flung at the boss, particularly for the decision to axe his stars for the young guns. Alan Hansen, providing one of the most famous quotes to have ever come out of the *Match of the Day* studio, said, 'I think they've got problems. I wouldn't say they've got major problems. Obviously, three players have departed. The trick is always buying when you're strong, so he needs to buy players. You can't win anything with kids.'

United rallied after that blip and registered five wins on the spin, including a 2-1 victory at champions Blackburn. The season's opener was soon forgotten as on 1 October, Cantona was cleared to play competitive football once again. The fixture that day saw Liverpool visiting Old Trafford. It was as if the fixture gods had transpired to bring this blockbuster to our lives. In true Cantona fashion, with collar up and chest pumped out, within two minutes the Frenchman had crossed for Nicky Butt to prod in at the far post before Liverpool struck back with two superb strikes from Robbie Fowler.

Then, as if the script had been written by Cantona himself, a penalty was awarded after Jamie Redknapp had bundled over Ryan Giggs in the area. It was a soft penalty for sure but Eric was certainly not going to let this opportunity pass and just a few strides later, David James was sent the wrong way and the number seven was back in the room. United kicked on and Cantona in particular was looking to make up for lost time. He scored 14 goals from October to May in the league, seven of them being match-winning strikes.

Kevin Keegan's Newcastle United had replaced Blackburn as the pretenders to the throne and were playing a brand of football at St James' Park that was nothing short of breathtaking. There was none of this 1-0 and shutting up shop – they were blowing teams away. Even when they struggled, they seemed to win by fine margins. If teams scored three, they would score four. It was quite extraordinary.

United had trailed the Magpies by 12 points as the calendar rolled into 1996. Showing the patience of a saint, they picked away at the lead as the Geordies slowly began to feel the pressure. Cantona again scored the only goal as United overturned Newcastle at St James' Park in March to wrestle back the advantage.

Keegan was a man on the edge and, like Hansen before him, he erupted in a tirade of words which would become famous the world over as the season drew towards its climax. With Ferguson hinting to the press that Leeds United only seem to turn up against his team in the final week, Keegan blew his fuse live on Sky Sports after his side had just beaten the Yorkshire side.

'No, no... when you do that with footballers, like he said about Leeds, and when you do things like that about a man like Stuart Pearce, I've kept really quiet, but I'll tell you something, he went down in my estimation when he said that,' roared Keegan. 'We have not resorted to that, but I'll tell you, you can tell him now if you're watching it, we're still fighting for this title, and he's got to go to Middlesbrough and get something, and... and... I'll tell you, honestly, I will love it if we beat them, love it!'

Newcastle could only draw at Forest and United beat Middlesbrough 3-0 on the final day to claim a third title in four seasons. Youngsters David Beckham, Gary Neville, Phil Neville and Nicky Butt had proved Hansen wrong. Cantona's goals had been pivotal in the run-in but he then saved his best for last as United faced old foes Liverpool in their third successive FA Cup Final. With the game edging towards extra time, Cantona volleyed in a half-clearance from James, who left an unguarded net. The ball seemed to travel through a plethora of bodies but none could stop the strike which flew into the goal to give United a second double in three years.

United again proved to be the team to beat at home on English soil. In Europe, though, it was a completely different affair as the three foreign player rule had completely hamstrung Ferguson's team. Having barely made it past the start line in any competition since the Cup Winners' Cup win in 1991, United had huffed and puffed but had not even threatened to blow a foreign shed down, never mind a house.

Teams in Spain and Italy had a large bias of domestic players. United, on the other hand, had a whole host of nationalities as the Welsh, Scottish and Irish lads were classed as foreigners. 'It's come two years late for us,' said Ferguson of the rule's abolishment, which meant that he had a full squad to choose from in the forthcoming 1996/97 Champions League campaign, 'because we'd have had a chance of winning the European Cup in 1994 otherwise.' A side-note to the summer of 1996 was that United had signed an unknown Norwegian called Ole Gunnar Solskjaer.

United meant business early on and a 4-0 drubbing of Newcastle in the Charity Shield lit the blue touchpaper on another season's work. An opening-day win over Wimbledon, who were then hosting games at Selhurst Park, seemed to be going the way of the form book. United were strolling in the summer sun, 2-0 up and looking to get off to a winning start to the campaign. Then out of nowhere and with the game ticking to a close, Beckham picked up the ball just a yard inside his own half, and unleashed a raking drive straight over the head of Neil Sullivan, who could only back-pedal towards his goal. The ball nestled into the empty net and on that very day, Beckham was truly announced to the world.

It wasn't all a bed of roses though for the Red Devils as revenge was served by Keegan's men at St James' Park when United were drubbed 5-0. Just days later, and with United still licking their wounds, they were again embarrassed down on the south coast. Southampton added to their woes and ran riot in a 6-3 bashing and the wolves were circling. Newspaper reports were that Ferguson was beginning to lose the dressing room and that the young players had run out of steam. This was not helped when United lost their third game on the spin, going down 2-1 at Chelsea.

Early exits in both domestic cups did nothing to help the cause, but for every mini crisis at Old Trafford there was always a response. The team went on a run of 17 games without defeat and again reached the top of the Premier League. The Champions League campaign was also going to plan. With a full team this time around United reached the semi-final, but Borussia Dortmund won both ties 1-0 to go through to the final.

United claimed another league title, this time quite comfortably. But what was probably the most shocking part to the end of the season was the decision by Eric Cantona to announce his retirement at the age of 30. It was rumoured that Cantona had told the manager just 24 hours after the defeat to Dortmund that he planned to retire in the summer. Eric released a statement. 'I have played professional football for 13 years, which is a long time,' it read. 'I now wish to do other things. I always planned to retire when I was at the top and, at Manchester United, I have reached the pinnacle of my career. In the last four and a half years, I have enjoyed my best football and had a wonderful time. I have had a marvellous relationship with the manager, coach, staff and players, and, not least, the fans. I wish Manchester United even more success in the future.'

United had crafted a system that worked beautifully for them with wingers who penetrated, spreading the pitch, and a forward line that had one player high on the last man and another playing in the hole. With that in mind, Ferguson replaced Cantona with Teddy Sheringham from Tottenham Hotspur. Sheringham was the perfect foil for Alan Shearer during England's run to the semi-finals of Euro '96 so would fit into the role of a number ten. Sheringham struggled initially but soon got into his stride as the team took top spot in the table after a 7-0 mauling of Barnsley in October 1997.

United would hold top spot for most of the 1997/98 campaign, until a rejuvenated Arsenal team hunted them down. The Gunners then went to Old Trafford and escaped with a 1-0 victory, their second of what would be a ten-game winning streak which would see the Premier League trophy head south for the first time in its existence. Another disappointing showing in Europe had added to what was a quite uneventful campaign for United. Ryan Giggs had missed large portions of the season with various injuries and Roy Keane had been on the treatment table for a prolonged period after his clash with Leeds's Alf-Inge Haaland.

The 1998/99 season began like any other. Signings were made to strengthen the squad as Ferguson had felt that his team was a little threadbare with injuries during the previous season's title-run in. Jaap Stam and Jesper Blomqvist were added to boost the numbers with Stam, signed to bolster a defence that was now missing the double act of Steve Bruce and Gary Pallister. Swedish winger Blomqvist had European experience and was an ideal replacement for Giggs when required.

Arsenal took the spoils in the Charity Shield, winning 3-0, and United fans must have been forgiven for thinking that Stam was going to be a dud. He was run ragged by Nicolas Anelka as the Gunners eased their way to victory.

United began their campaign at Old Trafford against Leicester City and trailed 2-0, so Ferguson turned to substitute Sheringham. Just moments after arriving on the pitch, Sheringham had pulled a goal back. Then in classic 'Fergie Time', David Beckham lifted the roof off Old Trafford with a 94th-minute equaliser from a sublime free kick that arced over the wall and into the bottom corner of the net.

It was a huge relief for Beckham who just weeks earlier had been vilified for his sending off during England's defeat to Argentina during the World Cup. The Stretford End chanted 'There's only one David Beckham' for the next few minutes as the winger made his way off the field. What was clear to Ferguson was that despite having Andy Cole, Teddy Sheringham and Ole Gunnar Solskjaer on his books, United were not quite firing on all cylinders as United drew 0-0 away at West Ham. All that was about to change as the boss brought in Dwight Yorke from Aston Villa. Yorke was of a similar style to Teddy, although younger and more mobile.

Yorke bagged a brace on his debut as United racked up their first three points of the campaign in a 4-1 win over Charlton. Another cherry on the cake was the return to first-team action for captain Roy Keane. His rehabilitation was complete and the midfielder was now starting to get some minutes into his legs. But just as United thought that they were getting their season going, another defeat to Arsenal derailed their mini revival.

United were sitting in tenth position and a title tilt was looking miles away as Arsenal were playing some fantastic football. The Champions League group phase had also begun and United had been drawn in the 'Group of Death' which contained Bayern Munich, Barcelona and Brondby. United had already battered Brondby during a pre-season friendly but found it tough going against both Barca and Bayern. All four ties ended in stalemate but with United scoring plenty against the team from Denmark, they managed to advance to the knockout stage at the expense of Barcelona.

As if the season could not get any tougher, United were drawn against Liverpool in the fourth round of the FA Cup. Michael Owen gave Liverpool an early lead but United showed a sign of things to come as two late goals turned the tie on its head and sent Ferguson's side into the next round. Middlesbrough had stunned Old Trafford with a 3-2 victory a week before Christmas, but that was to be the last present United gave away that season as they then ventured on a 33-game unbeaten run in all competitions.

Football has a funny way of bringing things together so it was almost inevitable that United would be drawn against Inter Milan and a certain Diego Simeone in the Champions League quarter-final. The Argentine, famous for his part in Beckham's dismissal at the World Cup, was sure to play an encore in this pantomime. He so nearly did. United raced into a two-goal lead at Old Trafford in the first leg thanks to assists from a pair of Beckham crosses. Simeone thought he had pulled a goal back only for the assistant referee to flag for pushing and spark enormous jeers from all four sides of the stadium. United then finished the job in Italy with a 1-1 draw and a 3-1 aggregate win.

Chelsea were taken to a replay in the FA Cup quarter-final before Dwight Yorke's brace at Stamford Bridge edged United over the line. Their reward was a semi-final with Arsenal. The Gunners were neck and neck with United in the league and in another tight encounter, the first match ended 0-0. The replay a week later was far from tame, however, as Beckham opened the scoring midway through the first half before Dennis Bergkamp equalised after half-time.

Roy Keane had already been booked when he lunged in on Marc Overmars late in the day. David Elleray had no hesitation on pulling out the yellow card, followed by a red, and pointing towards the tunnel. United looked dead on their feet and especially full-back Phil Neville so, with the game ticking towards full time, Ray Parlour drove at Neville inside the penalty box. Neville wearily dangled out a leg which caught the Arsenal winger and brought him to the ground.

Arsenal were awarded a penalty and with nearly the final kick of the game they had the chance to not only advance to a Wembley final, but also sway momentum in the title race. Bergkamp placed the ball on the spot. Schmeichel, who had saved a penalty against the Dutchman during the summer's World Cup, would need to guess correctly again to keep his team's chances alive. Bergkamp stepped up and hit a low shot to Schmeichel's left. The Dane parried the ball to safety, much to the delight of his team-mates and the travelling support at Villa Park.

Then in extra time, Ryan Giggs scored arguably one of the greatest goals in not only FA Cup history, but of all time. Patrick Vieira, tired and leggy, misplaced a long, square ball to the path of Giggs. The Welshman controlled it and began to run into the Arsenal half. Lee Dixon was side-stepped, and Martin Keown was shimmied past, followed by another side-step to make space away from Tony Adams, whose despairing lunge was too little too late as Giggs smashed the ball into the roof of the net, past England goalkeeper David Seaman.

The 2-1 victory against all odds galvanised United as they then turned their attention to winning back the title, and when Arsenal dropped points at Elland Road that opened the door for them to do that on the final day. United didn't disappoint as a stubborn Spurs side were eventually thwarted and the trophy was reclaimed. The Champions League Final had also been reached with United having beaten Juventus 4-3 on aggregate in what had been a titanic tussle. Level at 1-1 after the home leg, United needed to break their duck in Turin and record a first victory on Italian soil to go through.

Juve raced into a 2-0 lead but goals from Keane, Yorke and Cole sealed the deal as Ferguson and his men triumphed again against the backdrop of defeat. Keane, in particular, had dragged his team from the depths of despair to the brink of something quite spectacular. It had come at a cost as both Keane and Scholes would miss the final through suspension. Their performances that night belied the fact that they knew they would be out if United made it through. The team was the main priority, not individual merit.

The FA Cup Final against Newcastle United was a straightforward affair. Keane hobbled off during the opening exchanges and the man who replaced him, Sheringham, soon opened the scoring in a 2-0 win with Scholes claiming the other. United had won a third domestic double in the space of six seasons but the talk had turned to an unprecedented treble. Only domestic trebles had been achieved by teams across the continent but never with the biggest prize in club football thrown into the mix.

United lined up to face Bayern Munich in Barcelona's Nou Camp stadium with history in the offing. Schmeichel was in goal, behind a back four of Gary Neville, Denis Irwin, Jaap Stam and Ronny Johnsen. The midfield was makeshift as Beckham found himself playing in a central role with Nicky Butt while Giggs and Blomqvist occupied the wide areas. Yorke and Cole, who had been fantastic as a partnership, started up top. The two forwards had forged a great friendship off the field which had clearly yielded fruit as the pair had netted over 40 goals between them.

Bayern Munich took an early lead when a free kick by Mario Basler wrong-footed Schmeichel and opened the scoring for the Germans. Munich were devastating with their play and were unlucky not to extend their advantage when both crossbar and post were struck as Ottmar Hitzfeld's team turned the screw late on. United were barely able to sustain any amount of pressure and were struggling to string even the simplest of passes together.

Ferguson rolled the dice. Cole and Blomqvist were replaced by Sheringham and Ole Gunnar Solskjaer. Beckham moved back to the right and Giggs to the left, a much more natural fit. With stoppage time under way, United won a corner. Beckham's delivery caused mayhem in the Munich box as the ball pinged around. The presence of Peter Schmeichel had caused a level of panic for the German defenders as no one would have been allocated the Dane at set pieces. The ball eventually fell to Sheringham who swept it into Oliver Kahn's bottom-right corner.

United were back in business and as everyone was preparing to endure a further 30 minutes, Solskjaer won another corner. This time Schmeichel stayed back. Beckham swung in another pinpoint cross, which was flicked on by Sheringham, and Solskjaer, waving out his right leg, angled the ball into the Munich net. Two goals in two minutes meant United were champions of Europe. An historic treble had been achieved in the most dramatic of circumstances. This was further evidence of United's never-say-die attitude.

The following two campaigns were pretty straightforward domestically with both the 1999/2000 and 2000/01 seasons ending with United winning the Premier League and Arsenal again seen off as the rivalry intensified. A hat-trick of title triumphs then cemented United's dominance since the inception of the new-look top tier. The Intercontinental Cup was also won in 1999, although United failed in the 2000 World Club Championship, which they had entered instead of defending their FA Cup, much to the annoyance of the footballing fraternity. The Red Devils' excursions in the Champions League yielded just two quarter-final berths over the same period as they were unable to defend and then win back their title.

Luke Chadwick, a right-winger who had been signed as a 14-year-old schoolboy, remembers exactly what life at United was like at that time, 'I was on loan at Antwerp and was called back by the coaching staff. The manager told me that I was going to be around the first team from now on. Sir Alex Ferguson always took an interest in every player at the club, from the youth team through to the first team. That was the genius of the man.

'It was the same system right the way through the club. From under-14s up to 19s, the formation was ingrained in us so we all knew the way to play.'

Chadwick eventually broke into the first team and his few appearances contributed towards a title success in 2000/01. 'Every season we were expected to win the Premier League, minimum,' said Chadwick. 'In fact, we were told to win every trophy we played for.'

Rival teams had for a short period worked out a way to nullify the 4-4-2 system that Ferguson had created. Captain Keane was scathing in his criticism that the team had failed to build while on top. He felt that the squad was beginning to become stale, with the Premier League a shoo-in over the three seasons but United not being up to the high standards they had previously set in Europe. The boss had even flirted with a variety of different systems, none of which would herald any form of consistency.

The cracks were beginning to show in the dressing room as cycle two was starting to draw to a close. Beckham, who was now finding fame away from football, was left out of a match at Leeds United after reportedly failing to attend training due to his son being poorly. Jaap Stam was also in hot water with the boss as his autobiography, *Head to Head,* released in 2001 insinuated that the Scot had tapped up the Dutch defender while still at PSV. Such an act has always been illegal and with the book being serialised in several red-top papers, Ferguson moved swiftly to oust Stam, sending him to Italy and Lazio. Ferguson denied the claim.

'He'd been out for months and, when he came back, Steve McLaren and I thought he had lost a yard of pace,' said Ferguson. 'We played Fulham and he didn't have a good game, and at that moment Lazio come in and offer £16.5m. So then Jaap goes to Lazio and he played fantastic. So it was a bad decision. I should maybe have waited a bit longer.'

Ruud van Nistelrooy was signed in 2001 to bolster the forward line with Dwight Yorke seemingly falling out of favour over a string of events off the field. Van Nistelrooy was a lethal finisher and his signing was the beginning of the end for both Yorke and Cole. But the Dutchman's 36 goals in his maiden campaign were not enough to help United clinch a fourth successive title in 2001/02 as defensive frailties, after the departure of Stam, had exposed Ferguson's men. Arsenal, after three seasons of disappointment, had turned the tide and United could only muster a third-place finish, their lowest since the rebrand from the old First Division.

Denis Irwin and Ronny Johnsen then headed out of the door as the team began to evolve once more with Ferguson ringing the changes. His celebrated team of 1999 slowly but surely began to fade away. Peter Schmeichel, who had left for Sporting Lisbon directly after the Champions League win, was never really replaced as first Mark Bosnich was trusted between the sticks and then French international Fabien Barthez followed in 2000. The less said about Massimo Taibi the better. If you have never heard of the 'Blind Venetian' then I entrust you to use your local search engine and watch a video of his finest moments in a Manchester United shirt.

To tighten the leaking defence, the boss paid nearly £30m on Rio Ferdinand from rivals Leeds in the summer of 2002. The stylish defender strolled into Old Trafford with his bleached white, shaved hair, with a suit to match, and acted as if his whole life had been geared up for this moment. With van Nistelrooy firing at the top end, it was only going to take a stern defensive show and the team would be back to winning ways. The campaign got off to a shaky start but back-to-back defeats in December kick-started United and led them on to a run of 18 games unbeaten.

The title was heading back to Manchester in 2002/03 but there was some controversy along the way as Beckham and Sir Alex – the boss had been knighted in the wake of winning the Champions League in 1999 – had clashed following the FA Cup defeat to Arsenal. Ferguson, digging out the United number seven at full time, was not expecting a backlash from the England captain. Beckham was certainly not expecting his manager to leather a boot across the changing room, leaving him with a gash above his eye. Tensions were running high between the pair and at the end of the campaign Beckham moved to Spain with Real Madrid.

Cycle Three

Beckham's long-term replacement was an unknown Portuguese winger from Sporting Lisbon. United, having played a friendly against Sporting, soon realised the potential of the tricky teenager and a deal was struck. More players followed through the door as David Bellion, Tim Howard, Eric Djemba-Djemba, Gabriel Heinze and World Cup winner Kleberson all joined Cristiano Ronaldo at Old Trafford. It was a strange period for United in the transfer market. Players were brought in to build a squad, but none were what you would call superstars. This was a far cry from the star-studded unit of 1999.

The new recruits were blended with a sprinkling of academy players including the likes of John O'Shea, Darren Fletcher and Wes Brown, who were starting to become regular faces in the team. The manager still had the fight to keep going but his side was evolving and with Arsenal getting stronger, it was a tough ask to retain yet another title.

Just as Manchester United had hit their peak in 1999, Arsenal had been battling to keep in United's slipstream since their last title success in 1998. The 2001/02 win was a long time coming but with United's team slowly starting to tear at the seams, the Gunners' momentum was continuing to build, so much so that in the 2003/04 campaign, Arsène Wenger's men completed an historic achievement of winning the title without losing a single match. Their 38 fixtures ended with 26 wins and 12 draws. United could only watch on and admire the brand of football that Wenger had implemented in his half-decade in charge.

United would, however, not finish the season trophyless. A trip to Cardiff's Millennium Stadium and the FA Cup Final was their reward and plucky Millwall from the First Division – the second tier was renamed as the Championship that summer – were the lions in wait. Dennis Wise, player-manager of the lower division side, had tasted this experience before with unfancied Wimbledon. This time around the result went to script as United strolled to a 3-0 victory. Ronaldo opened the scoring on the verge of half-time before a second-half double from van Nistelrooy sealed the deal.

Ferguson opted to strengthen his attack again in the summer of 2004 as rising young star Wayne Rooney was brought in from Everton after a successful European Championship with England, even though he ended the tournament injured. Probably the strangest signing was that of Alan Smith from Leeds. Smith had captained his hometown club but could not stop them sliding out of the Premier League and into the second tier. Determined to regain control of the division, Ferguson had shuffled his pack. He continued to do so in the goalkeeping department as the boss was flicking between the American Tim Howard, and Northern Ireland international Roy Carroll.

The Portuguese influence was beginning to grow in the Premier League with Chelsea starting their own Iberian branch in west London. José Mourinho, fresh from leading Porto to the Champions League, was hired by the frivolous Russian owner Roman Abramovich. Mourinho wasted no time in bringing in his compatriots Ricardo Carvalho and Paulo Ferreira. The arrival of Mourinho in the Premier League signalled a massive shift in systems and formations. Mourinho would employ a 4-3-3 formation at Stamford Bridge that for two seasons, no other team in the country could get anywhere near.

The opening game of 2004/05 would see United head to Stamford Bridge in what was to be Mourinho's welcome party. United, still trying to find the solution to their recent dip in form, were humbled by the league's newcomer on day one. A 1-0 defeat for Ferguson was tough to take, even with an injury-ravaged side. The team on the pitch that day was

Howard, Silvestre, Keane, Neville, Fortune, Miller, O'Shea, Djemba-Djemba, Giggs, Scholes and Smith.

Speaking to a journalist after the game, Ferguson was quick to praise his makeshift team, 'I hoped for more from our possession, which we dominated, although our crosses were a bit scrappy and overhit. It was a good performance by us, we worked really hard, we can consider ourselves a bit unlucky. We had a lot of possession last year too and lost to a penalty so it's not been a good ground for us the last two seasons. But I'm confident in the ability of the team – I was before the match and I've no reason to think any differently after it.'

The faces on the pitch had changed but the principles and philosophy was still the same. United had ingrained in them a style of play that heralded back to the days of Sir Matt Busby and his legendary assistant Jimmy Murphy. United flattered to deceive in the league, finishing in third place. Arsenal were above them but it was Chelsea and Mourinho who were sitting pretty at the top of the pile. Mourinho's men had only tasted defeat once over a 38-game period and were worthy victors.

Chelsea had also edged United out of a place in the League Cup final by beating the Red Devils 2-1 on aggregate to advance to Cardiff. United were FA Cup holders and were in no mood to loosen their grip on that trophy. A successful route was undertaken to reach a second successive final where this time they would face Arsenal for another instalment of the fiercely contested rivalry.

Arsenal were looking for revenge as a shock 2-0 defeat at Old Trafford ended their record-breaking unbeaten run at 49. United were buoyed by the fact that they had seemingly turned a corner in the second half of the season and absolutely battered the Gunners in arguably one of the most one-sided finals I had ever seen. Unfortunately goals pay the rent. United couldn't find a way through and when Arsenal sensed it could well be their day, they hung on for a penalty shoot-out.

The Gunners dispatched all five of their attempts whereas Paul Scholes's miss was to be the damning moment of the day. Ferguson had seen enough from his side from January to May to realise that in fact he was heading in the right direction, although Chelsea at the time were seemingly buying any player who moved. The revolving door was nearly coming off its hinges at Stamford Bridge as new signing after new signing was made. Abramovich was clearly putting his money where his mouth was and Mourinho had absolutely no problems in helping him spend it.

In the summer of 2005, Manchester United were bought out by an American tycoon named Malcom Glazer. The NFL franchise owner had slowly built up his shares to the point that he was able to launch a takeover bid. This proved successful and by using Manchester United's own wealth, he was able to complete the purchase of possibly the richest football club on the planet. The sale instantly plunged United into debt to the tune of around £800m, although this figure varies depending on your favourite red top.

Despite the cashflow situation, Sir Alex strengthened as well. Edwin van der Sar was brought in from Fulham to be the first-choice goalkeeper as both Carroll and Howard had split the role with neither really excelling. The position had become a bit of a quandary for the boss, who had tried several players without limited success. Peter Schmeichel had big gloves to fill, but yet no one had even come close. Elsewhere, Ji-Sung Park was signed on the back of a decent World Cup in 2002 and added extra competition for the midfield places.

Phil Neville had now departed, moving down East Lancs Road to Everton, leaving only Ryan Giggs, Paul Scholes and Gary Neville as the remaining cast of the 1992 graduates. Wayne Rooney was now beginning to show why Ferguson had paid out more than £25m for the youngster with spectacular goals and assists beginning to light up every game. Cristiano Ronaldo, too, was becoming a force down the right-hand side of the pitch. His team-mates had urged the playmaker to stop throwing himself to the floor so easily and concentrate on his football. He was clearly listening.

The 2005/06 season got off to a decent start but this was soon cut short in the October when Roy Keane was stripped of the captaincy for his views during an interview on the in-house MUTV channel. Keane, whose turn it was to act as pundit for a game, didn't hold back on his comments after a 4-1 mauling at the hands of Middlesbrough. Ferguson was furious with Keane for throwing his team-mates under the bus. The programme was never aired in public and Keane felt that it was his time to leave.

The press were waiting outside the training ground with the news travelling fast round the country. Both men had a microphone thrust in their faces while heading off in their respective directions. 'Whilst it is a sad day for me to leave such a great club and manager I believe that the time has now come for me to move on,' said Keane. 'After so many years, I will miss everyone at the club.' Sir Alex was also full of praise for the Irishman, calling Keane 'the best midfield player in the world of his generation'.

When incidents happen at the club, the manager loved to circle the wagons. The siege mentality – we are Manchester United, we don't care about anyone else – was ingrained in the walls at the Cliff and Old Trafford. Call it arrogance, but United and particularly Ferguson, had a will to win despite what was thrown at them by outside forces. The players rallied domestically with a second-place finish. Chelsea again were on another level and finished comfortably ahead of United. The FA Cup was also a disaster as not only did United tumble out to rivals Liverpool, but a broken leg for Alan Smith compounded their misery.

Champions League success had not happened since lifting the trophy in 1999. A semi-final berth in 2001/02 flattered to deceive as United had gone out with a whimper in nearly every season since the victory in Barcelona. In 2005/06, a group that contained Benfica, Lille and Villarreal looked like a relatively easy path for United to navigate. They finished rock bottom. Rooney had seen red away to Villarreal in an opening that clearly set the tone for the whole group stage.

League Cup success was the silver lining to this season as United had fought their way to another Cardiff final, this time to face Wigan Athletic. United were in no mood for an upset with the league title seemingly well out of reach and a 4-0 rout courtesy of goals from Louis Saha and Ronaldo, coupled with Rooney's brace, put Wigan to the sword. The back story to this final was the omission from the starting line-up of Ruud van Nistelrooy. The Dutchman was the most lethal finisher I had ever seen at Old Trafford but he too, like Beckham, Keane, Stam and Yorke, had fallen foul of the boss.

Van Nistelrooy had reportedly had a training-ground bust-up with Ronaldo over his showboating during a crossing and finishing session. Van Nistelrooy was making the runs into the box, only for the ball to not be delivered, forcing the Dutchman to check back. The pair were split up by the coaching staff and reports of van Nistelrooy commenting on Ronaldo's father, who had recently passed away, were not welcomed. Ronaldo was the future. Ruud was not. He was on his way out of the door.

Two signings made in mid-season were Patrice Evra and Nemanja Vidic. The defenders were signed in January 2007 and were thrust into the back four with teething problems initially. Little did anyone know that the pair were about to become part of something pretty special.

The downside to the run-in was a 3-0 defeat at Stamford Bridge that handed Chelsea the title. United were outclassed that day but the most notable event was the injury to Rooney which led to his removal from the pitch. A broken metatarsal ended the forward's season prematurely but more importantly, England were potentially heading to the World Cup without their striker. Rooney recovered and was fit to play midway through the group stage, then came up against his club-mate Ronaldo as England faced Portugal in the quarter-final. During the second half, Rooney was dismissed in a Beckham-like scenario after stamping on Ricardo Carvalho. The referee was looking for a card and once the red was shown, Ronaldo acknowledged the moment with a wink, infuriating both Rooney and England. The Three Lions crashed out on penalties to Portugal and there were reports that Rooney and Ronaldo would not see eye to eye back at Old Trafford. How wrong those media stories were.

Sir Alex only made one signing in 2006, bringing in Michael Carrick from Spurs. The young midfielder was seen as an ideal replacement for Keane, whose departure had left a huge hole in the middle of the pitch.

Rooney and Ronaldo ran riot on the opening day of the season, demolishing Bolton Wanderers 5-1. They linked up beautifully with each other as well as each getting on the scoresheet, while the team had a better flow with the introduction of Carrick. A tall, silky player who could take the ball in tight areas and keep possession ticking over, Carrick was the ideal man to play alongside Scholes.

Ronaldo was becoming a more central figure in the team, playing either side of Rooney up top. The pair dovetailed in their play, with one going short and the other working the flanks. The partnership blossomed and United were in serious business. The football being played was fast and direct with the players at the top end of the pitch constantly interchanging with one another. Vidic and Evra had grown into their roles at the back and alongside

Ferdinand and Neville, they developed a remarkable understanding.

With goals coming from all areas of the pitch, it was no wonder that United were leading from the off. Chelsea were looking to claim a third successive title but Sir Alex had crafted another championship-winning team at Old Trafford. A 0-0 draw at Stamford Bridge all but secured the trophy and United were again to taste the champagne on the final day of the season. A 1-0 loss to West Ham couldn't dampen the spirits as the team celebrated in front of a full house.

The Red Devils had been resurgent in the Champions League as well as domestically, but AC Milan eventually ended their dream in the semi-final as a Kaka-inspired Rossoneri claimed a spot in the final against Liverpool. Wembley had finally been completed and was to host the 2007 FA Cup Final, where United faced Chelsea. The game was a tight affair with neither side really taking any chances. Extra time followed and when Ferdinand dallied over a ball behind allowing Didier Drogba to sneak in, Chelsea edged ahead and claimed the trophy with a 1-0 victory.

Rooney and Ronaldo had finished the campaign on an impressive 23 goals each, and the run continued for both men during the 2007/08 season. For some, the 1999 treble year is deemed the greatest in the club's history, but 2007/08 is arguably up there alongside it. Ronaldo was just sensational for United but his form came at a cost as his 42 goals had not gone unnoticed. Real Madrid were circling and it had been no secret that Ronaldo had a soft spot for the Spanish giants.

Ferguson had added another piece to the jigsaw over the summer with an audacious loan move for Carlos Tevez from West Ham. The Argentinian was an instant success at Old Trafford and scored some vital goals. The attacking options at the club were that of the class of 1999 era. Whereas that squad boasted Cole, Yorke, Sheringham and Solskjaer, this crop had Rooney, Ronaldo, Saha and Tevez. England international Owen Hargreaves was also signed from Bayern Munich to add a more defensive look to the midfield.

United were strong all over the pitch. They were playing some scintillating football and were bolstered further with the signings of youngsters Nani and Anderson. Chelsea were about to implode as Mourinho was sacked due to a variety of goings-on behind the scenes. United, sensing blood, took top spot in March and never looked back, although they needed to win on the final day of the season away to Wigan to wrap things up. Ronaldo scored a first-half penalty before Ryan Giggs's goal in the second half sealed the deal.

Back-to-back Premier League trophies had been won for the first time since 2000 and 2001. What was even more of a story was that both United and Chelsea had reached the Champions League Final. United lined up with van der Sar, Brown, Ferdinand, Vidic, Evra, Hargreaves, Scholes, Carrick, Ronaldo, Rooney and Tevez in from the off as the two Premier League big-hitters went toe-to-toe on a rain-soaked night in Moscow. Ronaldo pounced first to score a fine header, notching his 42nd goal of the season before Frank Lampard latched on to a slip in the rain from van der Sar and equalised on the stroke of half-time.

United were looking punch-drunk after an impressive opening 20 minutes. Chelsea were surging forward, wave after wave of attack and were unlucky not to take the lead when a Lampard shot struck the post and went away to safety. Extra time followed and again it was Chelsea in the ascendancy. United clung on and then in the game's first real flashpoint, a scuffle between Nemanja Vidic and Didier Drogba saw the Ivory Coast forward see red and miss the remainder of the match.

Weary and discombobulated, United were unable to make the extra man count and the game was set for penalties. Both teams began with successful kicks until Ronaldo missed with United's third effort. With the form the Portuguese forward had been in, you would have placed your mortgage on him scoring. His shot was weak and low to Petr Čech's right. The Chelsea stopper palmed his attempt away to safety. So it was advantage Chelsea right up until the final kick. Captain John Terry stepped up with a chance to claim the biggest club trophy in world football. Terry strode towards the ball but slipped at the vital moment, and his shot ricocheted off the outside of van der Sar's post.

United had a reprieve and Anderson opened the sudden-death kicks successfully. Salomon Kalou replied in kind for Chelsea, then Giggs – on the night he overtook Bobby Charlton's record as United's all-time record appearance-maker – scored. Nicolas Anelka, looking less than confident, was faced with a goalkeeper who was making himself as big as possible to fill his goal. Van der Sar was even pointing his finger as if to make a gesture towards the French forward as to which way to put the kick. Anelka began his run-up and with his right foot he placed his shot the same way as Ronaldo's. Van der Sar guessed correctly to get a decent hand on the effort and send the red half of the stands into sheer jubilation. United had become champions of Europe again and had done the Premier League/Champions League double for the second time in nine seasons.

The forward line was strengthened further with the signing of Dimitar Berbatov from Spurs early in the 2008/09 season, while Louis Saha would prove to be the fall guy and was eventually sold to Everton. United had the Super Cup and World Club Cup to look forward to, as well as defending their title and looking for a hat-trick of championships for the second time in a decade. Chelsea were hot on their heels in both the league and on the European scene. Brazil's 2002 World Cup-winning boss Luiz Felipe Scolari was brought in to take charge of the west Londoners as the longer-term replacement for Mourinho, whose role had been initially filled by Avram Grant to the end of the previous season.

First United took care of the Charity Shield, defeating FA Cup winners Portsmouth on penalties. Zenit St Petersburg took the spoils with a 2-1 success in the European Super Cup before United triumphed in the World Club Cup in Japan. Then it was the League Cup and another penalty shoot-out success, this time over Tottenham Hotspur at Wembley. Another trip to Wembley beckoned as the Red Devils met Everton in the FA Cup semi-final, but United's penalty success was about to come to a halt as the Toffees won the battle of wits from 12 yards. The Premier League was again added to the trophy cabinet at Old Trafford with Cristiano Ronaldo scoring 26 goals in all competitions.

The Champions League holders were again on the march to the final where this time they would face Pep Guardiola's Barcelona. Lionel Messi and co were also hitting their peak at the same time that United were flexing their muscles. Ronaldo had already signalled that this was to be his last appearance in a red shirt as his sights were well and truly set on a move to the Bernabéu. Ferguson's men never looked at the races and were soundly beaten 2-0 by the Catalan giants. It was a campaign that could have upstaged even the treble year of 1999. By contrast, it was no mean feat to win the Premier League, League Cup and World Club Cup. But they had come so close to winning the lot.

But what goes up must come down. United were attempting a record of three consecutive Charity Shield victories but were denied by Chelsea in the season's curtain-raiser, and Ronaldo had signed for Madrid for a world record £80m. As well as losing the Portuguese hot-shot, Carlos Tevez had also departed as a two-year loan from West Ham was completed and was the first sign of the Glazer era's frugalness. The option to sign was never taken up and Tevez decided that his future lay elsewhere. Across town, in fact, at Manchester City.

With two potent forwards leaving, the boss swooped in to sign free transfer Michael Owen. Owen in his prime was one of the most lethal finishers on the planet. The 2001 Ballon d'Or winner still had an eye for goal but had lost several yards of pace. Manchester City were building a team themselves and with a new-found wealth supporting their dream, Ferguson branded them the 'noisy neighbours'. Chelsea were having a change around and Scolari's spell was about to be brought to an abrupt end. Carlo Ancelotti was brought in to become the fourth manager in four years at the Bridge.

The Blues were galvanised and their new spirit and energy dislodged United from the summit of the table. United, despite Rooney's impressive haul of 34 goals, were blindsided when the forward was injured in mid-March and was unable to complete the title run-in. Berbatov was charged with the task of leading the line and while he did the job admirably, the absence of Rooney was glaringly obvious. United couldn't keep up with Chelsea and surrendered their crown in May 2010. The silver lining on the campaign was the retention of the League Cup, this time with a 2-1 win over Aston Villa.

Itching to get back on top, Ferguson bolstered his squad with the acquisition of Mexican striker Javier Hernandez. The 'Little Pea' – Chicharito – as he was known back home, was signed for an undisclosed fee. Whatever the outlay had been, it was immediately on the return as a goal in the Charity Shield victory over Chelsea ensured a winning start for both player and manager. United went top of the league in November following a 7-1 demolition of Blackburn Rovers in which Berbatov had scored five of the goals.

The Red Devils would have to wait until February when they suffered their first defeat of the campaign, with Wolverhampton Wanderers taking the points despite Nani scoring in the opening exchanges. Further defeats to Chelsea, Liverpool and Arsenal followed but with United having already done the donkey work in the first two-thirds of the season, the league title again found its way back down Sir Matt Busby Way.

Again United had charged to the Champions League Final, their third in four seasons, again finding themselves against Pep Guardiola's impressive Barcelona. The pre-match build-up was that of United at Wembley in 1968 and the victory over Benfica only a decade after the Munich air disaster. The romance of the return to the twin towers was poured on by all angles but Barcelona had history of their own there with a 1-0 victory over Sampdoria in 1992.

Rooney played in the hole behind Chicharito, hustling his way between Barca's midfield and defence. The problem for United was that the midfield two of Carrick and Giggs were completely outclassed on the day by Busquets, Xavi and Iniesta. And then there was the devastating form of Villa, Pedro and Messi in attack. Speaking to the press after the 2-0 final defeat in 2009, Sir Alex had said, 'They get you on that carousel and they make you dizzy with their passing.' The same was to happen just two years later. Barcelona scored first through Pedro with Rooney equalising ten minutes before half-time, but Messi and Villa rounded off what would turn out to be a pretty one-sided affair and wrap up a 3-1 win.

Ferguson's 4-4-2 had still overcome all the teams in both the Premier League and on the European scene, Barca aside. This Barcelona team is arguably one of the greatest club sides to have ever played the game. The fact that Sir Alex had kept his system almost identical for all these years just shows that you can play your own way and still get results. All this came at a time when 4-2-3-1 was the new fashion of the footballing world. Teams were starting to pack their midfields to gain superiority in the centre of the park.

Across town, Manchester City were slowly beginning to build momentum under the tutelage of Roberto Mancini. Carlos Tevez was in devastating form and was forming a deadly partnership with his fellow countryman Sergio Agüero, although United began the 2011/12 campaign in good nick including an 8-2 demolition of Arsenal at Old Trafford.

The Theatre of Dreams seemed to be raining goals as just a few games later and with United unbeaten, City rolled into town and absolutely destroyed the Red Devils in front of their own supporters. Jonny Evans was given his marching orders early in the second half and with City smelling blood, they wrapped up the afternoon by firing six goals past David de Gea. What ultimately hurt United the most, although they couldn't have known it at that point, was that on the final day of this topsy-turvy season they would lose the title on goal difference.

United were in the driving seat as the season went on and were in control of the title race until a blip at home to Everton. Leading 4-2 with 15 minutes remaining, Ferguson's men played in the only way they knew how, by going for the jugular. Patrice Evra was close to making it 5-2 but rattled the crossbar and before United could say Premier League title, Tim Cahill and Steven Pienaar had combined to pull the Toffees level. City would capitalise a week later with a 1-0 home win in the derby.

On the final day, United beat Sunderland 1-0 at the Stadium of Light to almost confirm themselves as champions of English football again. City had started the day top of the table but were still playing and losing 2-1 at home to Queens Park Rangers. Edin Dzeko equalised on the stroke of 90 minutes and with the clock ticking and time still to play, they had hope. Cue the immortal line from Martin Tyler as the ball broke kindly in the box to Agüero from Mario Balotelli's pass. The Argentine took one touch and lashed the ball past a hapless Paddy Kenny.

United had lost the title with virtually the last kick of the season. While Mancini and his players danced on the pitch in delight, Ferguson and his charges were left to lick their wounds up in Sunderland. Speaking to Sky Sports, Sir Alex said, 'You don't know what can happen in the extra two minutes, but they got that break and won the game. It is a cruel way to have the title ripped away, but I've had a lot of ups and downs in my 25 years here. It won't happen again.'

If the cycles had taught us anything, it was that when a new-found assault on the league was forthcoming, Sir Alex would bring in a striker to take them on to the next level. Robin van Persie was signed from rivals Arsenal, who had failed to keep hold of their talisman after contract talks stalled. The United boss wasted no time and brought in the Dutchman to follow in the footsteps of fellow countryman Ruud van Nistelrooy. Van Persie got off to a flyer and notched on his home debut against Fulham, then followed up with a hat-trick in the 3-2 victory over Southampton after United had found themselves two goals down.

The team had the bit between their teeth in 2012/13 and were victorious against Liverpool, Chelsea, Arsenal and City. Van Persie was instrumental in all of the wins, not least with an 89th-minute free kick to win the derby at the Etihad. City were not as fluent as the previous campaign and by the time the two teams met again in March, United held a commanding 15-point lead. City would take revenge at Old Trafford but by the time that van Persie headed back to north London for the final match of April, United had already comfortably wrapped up the title. The *piece de resistance* was a hat-trick from the Dutchman in a 3-0 home win over Aston Villa to confirm the championship. The Red Devils were then given a guard of honour by the Gunners, much to the dislike of the Arsenal fans who had felt that van Persie had engineered a move away from the club despite being their captain.

Van Persie relished the walk on to the pitch and being applauded by the players of which he had shared a dressing room just ten months earlier. To rub salt into the wounds of all those in the home end of the stadium, he again notched to silence the boos that rang out on his every touch. The jeers soon turned to cheers as Swansea City came to town to partake in Sir Alex Ferguson's final home match as Manchester United manager. His team that day was David de Gea, Phil Jones, Rio Ferdinand, Nemanja Vidic, Patrice Evra, Danny Welbeck, Michael Carrick, Paul Scholes, Shinji Kagawa, Robin van Persie and Javier Hernandez.

Hernandez had set the tone for the afternoon by firing United into a first-half lead but Swansea, who clearly had not read the script, manufactured an equaliser through the Spaniard Michu. United huffed and puffed and, like a thousand times before this day, had played until the death and with the game moving into the closing moments, a corner at the Stretford End was swept in by Rio Ferdinand to take the roof off the stadium.

The boss had finished his final home game with a flourish as in true Sir Alex Ferguson style, his teams just never knew when to quit. Over 26 years of managing one of the biggest football clubs in the world, even with the pressure of his early years, the boss knew his style and how it was going to play out. The personnel would change but the philosophy would not. It would be 4-4-2 with fast, attacking football with width the order of the day. An unconventional front line would always consist of a striker and a playmaker who liked to drop deep. It worked and then some.

Even until the end, playing against the likes of AC Milan, Barcelona and Real Madrid, Ferguson stuck to his guns. Sometimes he didn't get the success that the performances merited but he never wavered. His honours will go unmatched for a long time to come. His legacy is his 4-4-2 and attacking brand of football. It didn't work every time, but when does it? Manchester United fans had 26 years of highs and lows. They wouldn't change that for the world.

7

Wimbledon
The Crazy Gang

Crazy
adjective: mad, especially as manifested in
wild or aggressive behaviour

'WE WERE the Cinderellas of the FA Cup,' recalls Bobby Gould, the manager who led Wimbledon to their crowning glory. Saturday, 14 May 1988, was to be the absolute pinnacle in the club's history. Not only did they manage to win the FA Cup, which in itself is no mean feat, but in doing so they defeated Liverpool, derailing the Reds' efforts to record a league and cup double. The trophy win was the peak of an 11-year rise from the depths of the Southern League to the twin towers at Wembley. If you believe that miracles could only happen in the movies, then look no further than down at SW19 for some reality.

The side-note to this upwardly moving fairytale is that in reaching their Everest, Wimbledon played what purists would call 'anti football'. The long-ball label was attached to the Dons during their march through the lower leagues towards the summit, but there seems to be a huge difference between a long aimless ball up the field and a well-worked long-range pass. Wally Downes, a former player and later manager of AFC Wimbledon, said, 'There's a massive snobbery if you play the ball long, opposition fans start booing and you get pigeon-holed as "they're just a boot it team". It's a load of nonsense.'

Gould had inherited a squad with a strong work ethic and a camaraderie that not many teams seem to be able to recreate in today's current football climate. Much of the groundwork had been laid for Gould by his predecessor, Dave Bassett. The man known as 'Harry' had steered the club from the old Fourth Division to the First Division with three promotions coming in a whirlwind four-season period. Bassett had installed a 'Crazy Gang' mentality among his players. Unlike any other team written about in this book, Wimbledon had their own style to accompany their 4-4-2 system. Many didn't like it, but for those who were among it, let's just say that practice makes perfect.

The beginning of the golden age for Wimbledon began in the mid-1970s. While still operating in the non-league pyramid, a heroic FA Cup run in 1974/75 captured the imagination of the country as the Dons became the first team outside of the Football League to eliminate a team from the top division. Burnley were the unlucky recipients that day. But Wimbledon's headline-grabbing didn't stop there as reigning champions Leeds United were waiting in the next round. A heroic display at Elland Road ensured that the match ended in a 0-0 draw and a sell-out crowd crammed in at Selhurst Park to witness the non-league side depart after a narrow 1-0 defeat in the replay.

With new-found belief around the club and a collection of street-smart amateur footballers, Wimbledon won the Southern League for three consecutive seasons from 1974/75 to 1976/77, before inevitably they were elected into the Fourth Division. Chairman Ron Noades had begun a campaign for the club to be given the chance to participate at Fourth Division level. Eventually, the hierarchy could no longer afford to ignore the clamour.

The march towards the Football League had begun with Allen Batsford at the helm. Batsford had joined the club in 1974 and quickly realised the exact type of players he would need to get him out of the non-league battleground. Playing for the boss as part of the push for full-time football was Bassett, who had a great relationship with the manager and his hard graft in central midfield had helped the team achieve their goal. At the end of the 1976/77 campaign, Batsford had finally taken Wimbledon to the promised land. Or that's what the fans who attended the Plough Lane stadium thought. After a whole history of playing non-league football, how much better could it really get? Bassett, later in manager form, and Gould were about to show them.

So what do Bassett House, Lawrie House and Batsford House all have in common? They are all apartment blocks built on what was the old Plough Lane ground. Wimbledon's former home had always been something of an enigma. To some it was a run-down little shack of a place but to others, it was home. Football journalist Patrick Barclay said, 'It's evocative. Not to be written off as "homely". A very good place to watch football. I loved Plough Lane, probably because the journalistic facilities were as good as they could manage, so most of us did. Happy memories.'

The stadium was home to the Dons between 1912 and 1991, but its time was up as a result of the Taylor Report issued in 1990 following the tragedy at Hillsborough in 1989. An FA Cup semi-final between Liverpool and Nottingham Forest held at Sheffield Wednesday's stadium brought about one of the worst sights ever witnessed at a football match on English soil as 96 fans lost their lives as a result of the events on that fateful day due to crushing and overcrowding. We pray that no one ever has to go through anything like that ever again. The report read that all top-flight stadia should be all-seated by the end of the 1994 campaign. With Wimbledon struggling financially and the stadium falling into a state of disrepair, it was agreed that a ground share with Crystal Palace would provide a temporary solution.

As well as this, the stadium had been through a catalogue of bizarre events. Bombing during World War Two had left the ground in a bad way. It was damaged so badly that the club were not permitted to charge for entry during games over that period. This did not deter any of the supporters who clamoured for their football fix while the heroes abroad fought for our freedom. In an attempt to recoup some funds after the war, Wimbledon applied to run a market from the land. This was swiftly denied by the local authority as a statute placed by Charles

I in 1628 prevented any markets to be in place within a seven-mile radius of Kingston upon Thames. Plough Lane, unfortunately, fell just inside this bracket. Club chairman Sydney Black purchased the freehold on the stadium in 1959 for just over £8,000 from Merton Borough Council. The problem with this was that it came with a condition stating that if the site was ever to be used for any purpose other than sport, the council would have the right to buy the ground back for the same price it had been purchased at, regardless of inflation. The value of the stadium could never grow above the £8,000 paid.

In 1983, the club bought out the clause for around £100,000 and during times of financial hardship, they sold it on again to chairman Sam Hammam for £3m. It was an enormous amount considering how much Mr Black had acquired it for. Sadly for the club, the funds were never found to carry out the necessary repair work and the stadium and surrounding land were eventually sold to developers. I digress slightly with a brief but warm introduction to the ground on which this footballing miracle would be played out. It was fitting that during its swansong as a footballing theatre, the glory years which concluded a lifetime of uncertainty and disdain would entwine into the tapestry of this magnificent fairytale.

The 91 other Football League teams were clearly not ready for what was about to be bestowed upon them. To rival supporters, it was a way to taunt and mock the club for its approach to games. For the following of the blue and yellow, it was a system that worked beautifully for the players that were brought into the side. Wimbledon were going to upset the aristocracy, and they loved every minute of it.

Their inaugural Football League season in 1977/78 begun with a pretty entertaining 3-3 draw at home to Halifax Town, but a last-minute equaliser meant that the Dons would have to wait for their first win. According to the book written by Bassett and Downes, *Crazy Gang*, Batsford described the match as 'disgraceful'. Bassett added, 'I'm sure the crowd of 4,616 enjoyed the momentous occasion, and a six-goal thriller. The goals we conceded were shit though.'

Wimbledon's opening game heralded the line-up of Dickie Guy, Jeff Bryant, Dave Galvin, Dave Donaldson, Glenn Aitken, Geoff Davies, Steve Galliers, Willie Smith, Roger Connell, Billy Holmes and John Leslie. These are names that will be remembered by supporters of an older persuasion. Captain Bassett was suspended for the opening of the campaign but would soon return to action, while Bryant holds the accolade of becoming the first player to register a goal for the club in the Football League. Despite the all-action start, Wimbledon would have to wait for seven games to pass before registering their first victory. A better late than never performance saw the team swat aside Northampton Town.

The leap from non-league to a more intense format would take its toll on the Dons as they had continued to operate on a part-time basis. A mid-table finish of 13th was achieved and although it was perceived to be respectable in some parts, to those closer to the club, there was slight disappointment. The footballing fraternity was also beginning to become averse to the team's approach. Bassett said, 'We failed to win many friends; after a draw against Darlington, their manager Peter Madden described us as "the worst side I have ever seen for conning the ref". What a load of crap.'

Some of the togetherness in the squad was brought about by not having as much talent as others but making the best out of what you had. Batsford once said, 'We had terrific spirit but no money. Because a team bus cost too much, Ron ordered the players to drive to Rochdale, just like a pub side.' Bassett stated in *Crazy Gang*, 'Mind you, even when we did have a bus, like on that trip to Swansea, it could be a shambles – we left Dave Galvin behind at the service station and he missed the match!'

Outspoken chairman Ron Noades had clashed with Batsford during the course of the season, which wasn't an ideal scenario to have in the backdrop of your debut campaign at Fourth Division level. Eventually the butting of heads led to the departure of the much revered Batsford and January 1978 would see the man who had been instrumental in the rise be replaced by Dario Gradi. Another change was to the captaincy. Bassett, a lieutenant under Batsford, had to surrender the armband to incoming record signing Les Briley. Was Bassett bitter? Of course he wasn't. Bassett said to the press that Briley 'had signed from Hereford the previous season – they were a Second Division team at the time, so he was quality'.

Bassett was coaching as well as playing but with his playing days dwindling down, he assisted Gradi with his duties. Gradi tried to play in a more 'footballing' kind of fashion, and for a time it seemed to work. A third-place finish meant that in their second full season, Wimbledon had won promotion to the Third Division, aided by more than 20 goals from Alan Cork. With the 1970s nearing its conclusion, Wimbledon had already won three league titles during the decade and had been promoted twice. Bassett had been directly involved in all of the goings on both on and off the field. The club was certainly on the up, but with a budget of shirt buttons and attendances still bordering on non-league, it was only a matter of time before the Dons would hit their glass ceiling.

A mass of players had left the club due to its commitment to full-time status. Many of them were still in full-time employment and were unable to give that up to continue the club's journey. The upheaval of players and advancement of league and standard had taken its toll on the Dons and they suffered the disappointment of relegation as the team finished rock bottom of the Third Division. The 1979/80 season was a blot on the copy book of the last half-decade but sometimes in life you have to take a step back to work out how to move forward. Wimbledon as a club did exactly that. And while relegation to some was a bitter pill to swallow, to others, it was a chance to roll up their sleeves and get stuck in for a trademark example of what was to follow.

Ron Noades had decided that his future lay elsewhere and decided to purchase Crystal Palace from across town. As the new year chimed into 1981, manager Dario Gradi followed suit and headed east to Croydon. Bassett was given the reins and with the Dons in touching distance of the promotion places, they embarked on a 12-match unbeaten run. Bassett, speaking outside the training ground, said, 'Off Dario went with Ron to Selhurst and it was down to me, and then came that 12-match unbeaten run. The players were brilliant, especially given all the off-the-field shenanigans. They just got on with their jobs, gave their all, and churned out the results.'

With the run eventually coming to an end, the players dusted themselves down and got back on the horse. Again, this was part of the make-up among the squad as a whole. The football played, though, was a war of attrition. Several times in the lead-up to the season's finale, the Dons ran out 1-0 winners. Score a goal and defend like lions. It wasn't pretty, but who cares when you are grinding out results? You don't get trophies for fancy football, although you do get promoted if you finish in fourth position after a string of victories. A different manager but the same outcome and after four seasons in the Football League, Wimbledon had won promotion again and marched back to the Third Division.

The team played in a direct fashion, but it was no 'hit and hope' scenario. Glyn Hodges, a player signed by Gradi as an apprentice, knew that there was more method behind that style of play than just shelling the ball up the pitch. 'Your first target would be a long ball from your final third to their final third,' he said. 'I don't know if these are the correct figures, but you had to hit that 100 times, and if the winger collected it 40 times he would get in 12 crosses and, from that, you would score two goals. This is how it was sold to us. It was a science that worked. We had to play that way, and that is how we won games.'

This team was now Bassett's. Hodges had emerged into the first team along with another apprentice graduate, Wally Downes. 'Harry and Dario were totally different,' said Hodges. 'From how they were as people right through to their coaching sessions. Dario would have all the cones lined up – all crop circles and drills – while Harry would have us playing a game called "Harryball", where anything could go. But he was good at the tactical side.'

Downes began on £5 a week. Some people would say that was good money back then. Your grandad maybe, while reminiscing about taking your grandmother to the pictures and still having change for the bus home. By the time Downes signed his papers, £5 was of little use to anyone. But his sheer determination to become a professional footballers drove him on.

Bassett had a functional style of play where every single player must have known their role and responsibility. 'We worked a lot on functional 11 v 11 work,' said Downes. 'This can be a little bit stop-start with the coach driving home his points, but Harry was a smart teacher and used to build the sessions culminating in a game that could flow with the information still fresh.

'Instead of finishing with a small-sided game we finished with 11 v 11 that was very competitive. The squads were much smaller then and players were more willing and adaptable because of this.' Because of this attention to detail, the squad, albeit a small one, was tight-knit and understanding of what was required.

Despite being well organised and having a squad more like brothers than co-workers, sometimes the footballing gods and life itself can conspire against you. The 1981/82 season certainly dished out its fair share of dark moments to sort the Wimbledon equilibrium back into kilter. For every red card that season, and there were a few, another slice of bad luck followed. Alan Cork, the goalscoring linchpin, broke his leg in the autumn of the campaign, and with a miserly two points collected from a possible 27, it was always going to be an uphill task. This was also after the introduction of three points for a win. The players would have to wait until the tenth game of the season to eventually pick up their win bonuses, if the club could even afford to pay them.

Another relegation followed with the Dons never really hitting their stride and eventually finishing 21st, despite a late rally towards the end of the season. Without doubt the lowest point of the season was the passing of new signing Dave Clement. Clement had signed from QPR and had only managed a dozen or so appearances before a broken leg at Doncaster Rovers curtailed his season. The injury clearly had a big impact on Clement, a player in the twilight of his career, and on 31 March 1982 he took his own life. God rest your soul, Dave.

But out of the darkness cometh the light and those dark days were about to have a whole new glow around them. Bassett was disappointed but focused on a swift return to the Third Division. Wimbledon had stuck by him whereas in this day and age a trigger-happy board would have got rid of him. There can be a lot said about how comfortable continuity can be for players and staff. Players can be creatures of comfort and habit. Bassett knew that there was hard work ahead. 'I invented "Harryball", where a player was asked to dribble through several grids with the ball and the rules were there were no rules,' said Bassett. 'That caused a few skirmishes. I would often call them in for Sunday training. We had laughs, but when we were working we were fucking working.'

There's an old saying that 'hard work beats talent, when talent doesn't work hard'. Now don't get me wrong, I am not for one moment accusing any of these Wimbledon players of not having any talent; far from it in fact. To even make it to the Football League is far beyond the dreams of pretty much every schoolkid in the land. But the hard graft that was instilled into this team would surpass anyone they would face over a season and it paid dividends in 1982/83 as the Dons bounced back to the Third Division with an 11-game unbeaten run. Bassett had momentarily switched to a sweeper until defeat to Bristol City, who were at the foot of the table, prompted him to switch things around.

'We flirted with the sweeper system with me as a sweeper after the '82 World Cup,' said Downes. 'We went 12 games unbeaten and got to Bristol City at the top of the table. We had a player sent off and lost 4-2 and Harry changed from a possession and passing team to a direct high pressure team. He explained his reasoning showed us his vision and we bought into it. Teams hated playing against us because of our work rate and the pressure we put them under. Not all of us enjoyed playing that way, but we were a team and played for each other.'

An excerpt taken from *Crazy Gang* explained Bassett's decision to switch from the trialled sweeper system, 'To put it bluntly, what I then did was to rip up my tactics book, axing the sweeper system that had at one time worked so well for us. We had a meeting and implemented total change – for everyone in the club. From now on we would be considerably more direct, getting the ball in the opposition penalty area. It wasn't music to their ears at first, especially the midfielders, players like Downes and Hodges, but it was reluctantly accepted.'

At that time the technical director at the FA was a man named Charles Hughes. Hughes was a massive adversary of the long-ball game and had preached this into his coaching syllabus for many years. He called it the 'POMO' theory. From his statistical analysis, Hughes emphasised the importance of particular areas of the field from where goals were most often scored. He called these areas the 'POMO' – Positions of Maximum Opportunity – and asserted that players would score if the ball was played into them enough times. Hughes stressed the importance of set plays and crosses into the penalty area.

Of course this was frowned upon by the fans and players from footballing royalty. For every long, aimless ball played into a channel, there was also a Glenn Hoddle to beautifully weave his way through a crowded defence to score. It's all about balance. For Wimbledon, who didn't have the luxury of a Hoddle or Keegan, they had to cut their cloth accordingly. 'We were all aware of our roles and responsibilities from training ground scenarios,' said Downes. 'We trained a lot longer than players do nowadays and were more resilient. In the final third it was all about getting good delivery into the box at the optimum speed.

Players had to attack various areas of the box and wide men concentrated on hitting the areas as opposed to picking people out. We were never encouraged to foul anywhere on the pitch as set plays were an opportunity for the opposition to score, or if in the opposition half, an opportunity to rest, relax and regroup.'

What followed was sheer jubilation as the Dons went from a season of sadness and misfortune to a period of dominance and ecstasy. They not only bounced back to the Third Division at the first time of asking, but also cruised to the league title following a 22-game unbeaten run, culminating in a 3-1 victory over Bury on the final day. A young full-back by the name of Nigel Winterburn was added to the squad. He would prove to be a snip at around £15,000.

The 1983/84 season continued in the same vein as the previous outing. If it isn't broken then don't fix it, although Downes did say that the players 'adapted slightly' as they crept up the leagues. With the Dons seemingly on the verge of a second promotion in a row, just one win was needed from the final two ties. A home match to Gillingham had the fans biting their nails, but at the same time they were hoping for what would be a party post-match. It was to be a false start as despite taking an early lead, Wimbledon found themselves 2-1 down from goals by Tony Cascarino and Steve Bruce. With portable radios in hand, the crowd at Plough Lane seemed to pick up slightly as news filtered through that Sheffield United had tasted defeat at Bolton and Wimbledon had done it. Alan Cork had returned from his broken leg at the tail of the title-winning season

Diego Simeone giving the thumbs up to his hard-working players

Derby defeat Benfica on a historical night at the Baseball Ground

Clough and Taylor look on as Forest edge towards a European Cup Final

Wenger lifts the Premier League trophy as Arsenal join the 'Invincibles'

Brazil claim the 1994 World Cup despite the unrest back home regarding the tactics of the coach

Sanchez scores a first-half header to rock Liverpool and to land Wimbledon the FA Cup

United claim the treble of Premier League, FA Cup and Champions League after a topsy turvy match in Barcelona

Sacchi being held aloft after leading his AC Milan side to more honours

Vardy breaks the Premier League record for goals scored in consecutive matches, which still stands

Leeds United, First Division champions. The last team to win the top flight coached by an Englishman

Liverpool securing yet another prize at their second home Wembley. This time the Charity Shield

Everton line up in the Cup-Winners' Cup Final in Rotterdam in a historical campaign

and absolutely blew away the Third Division's back lines, finishing with an impressive haul of over 30 goals.

Consolidation is normally a key word in any newly promoted team's vocabulary. With Wimbledon having had four years of bouncing between divisions, it was no surprise that managing to achieve a second promotion in three seasons would have many round the club fearing that the leap from Fourth Division to Second would prove too great. There were still some big teams kicking about in the second tier of English football and the Dons were rubbing shoulders with the likes of Manchester City, Wolverhampton Wanderers, Crystal Palace and Leeds United.

A double over London rivals Palace and some impressive wins including a 5-0 home triumph against Sheffield United ensured a healthy 12th-place finish. What was more significant at the time was that the club had paid out £30,000 for Lawrie Sanchez from Reading. The 25-year-old midfielder had been forging a decent reputation for himself and managed to notch five goals in the final 20 games of the season.

The 1985/86 campaign was to see yet another upturn in the crazy world of Wimbledon. Clearly not fazed by the 'bigger boys' around them, the Dons set about swashbuckling their way through the division. To add to the madness, Wimbledon actually won their opening game of the season for the first time in about 20 years. Another league double came over neighbours Palace, and they did the same to Fulham as well for good measure. In fact the London derbies were kind to Wimbledon with wins also coming against Charlton Athletic. Bassett said, 'We were on a roll. Could little old Wimbledon make it to the First Division? Too bloody right we could.'

Bassett had assembled a good squad on a tight budget. The players knew the system and exactly what the manager required from them and if they didn't, then they would certainly know about it. Daniel Taylor, writing for *The Guardian* in 2015, stated, 'It might not fit into the stereotype of this homespun club, where the players stole traffic cones for what passed as a training ground and there was an annual trip to Magaluf, but their manager was ahead of Opta and Prozone by roughly 20 years.'

'Billy Beane at Oakland came in with *Moneyball* and all the statistics,' Bassett said. 'We were doing that in 1981.' For anyone not familiar with the *Moneyball* story, a small-town baseball club going nowhere and working with only a fraction of the budget against the likes of the New York Yankees decided to buck the trend and sign players on their statistical analysis rather than the old-fashioned way of big names. The outcome was extraordinary and the team became the first in baseball history to win 20 games in a row.

With the Dons in the hunt for promotion to the First Division, more strengthening was made with John Fashanu being signed from Millwall. Fash had terrorised their back line earlier in the campaign. George Graham, then Millwall's manager, had requested around £150,000 for the striker, although Bassett had managed to knock down the price to £125,000. It would be a bold signing. Downes said, 'Fash had told Harry before signing he wanted nothing to do with our famed Crazy Gang antics.' Fashanu's goals and performances towards the end of the season were valuable. Also added to the squad was 18-year-old Dennis Wise who, according to Downes, could 'start a fight in an empty house' but as with the rest of the squad, he had qualities, even at such a young age, that Bassett would love.

With three games away from home to complete the campaign, a trip to Leeds Road, Huddersfield, was the first chance to get over the line and join the English elite. Saturday, 3 May 1986 was yet another landmark day in Wimbledon's history as a 1-0 win proved enough and clinched third place and promotion to the First Division. Sanchez scored to seal the victory and claimed afterwards, 'It's probably the most important goal I'll ever score.'

Wimbledon's left-back had been claiming all the plaudits for his performances that season. Nigel Winterburn had quickly earned a reputation as a no-nonsense full-back who would go on marauding runs down the flank, proving to be another great example of good business by Bassett.

And on to the First Division. Four promotions in a five-year spell had started to erase the days of playing Southern League football from the memory, although as a club, you should never forget where you come from. The 1986/87 season would see the likes of Manchester United, Liverpool and Arsenal come to town. Heady days at Plough Lane which had only a decade earlier hosted Waltham, Ealing and the like.

The step up in class meant that again the squad would need bolstering. Vinnie Jones, a midfielder who was playing for non-league Wealdstone, was pointed out to Bassett by old friend Batsford. Taking the judgement of his friend and mentor on board, Bassett paid £10,000 for Jones. The contract negotiations were swift, not drawn out through agents like they are nowadays. Bassett said in *Crazy Gang*, 'During talks with Vinnie I told him he'd be on £150 a week, plus £50 a goal and £50 per appearance in the first team. Then I told him, "That's it. See you tomorrow." Vinnie loitered, so I asked, "What's up?" He replied something like, "Any chance of a signing-on fee?" I told him, "No. Now fuck off."'

Belief was flowing through the squad and in their first outing at the top table of English football the Dons finished a very respectable sixth. This included a double over Manchester United and a 2-1 win at Liverpool. The team had continued with the same style and philosophy as when they had played in the Fourth Division. The personnel was beginning to change but the ideology would continue. Wimbledon played a 4-4-2 like no other team mentioned in this book. In fact, it was the 4-2-4 when in possession that bamboozled teams. They just couldn't cope with the Dons' fitness levels. Despite criticism from the press and other quarters, you don't reach the top six of English football by being a rubbish team, so something was clearly working. Cruelly for Wimbledon, had it not been for the ban placed on English clubs at the time, they would have been playing in the UEFA Cup the following season.

The 1987/88 campaign was to be the 'flag pole dug into the peak of the mountain' moment. With the club aiming for another stab at upsetting the applecart, a bombshell was dropped in the summer of 1987. With owner Sam Hammam attempting to undermine Bassett, a clash of heads led to

Bassett handing in his notice and heading round the M25 to Watford. The club moved swiftly to replace him and brought in Bobby Gould with his assistant, Don Howe. The players were relieved that Howe had been part of the setup as he was revered around the country as being a top coach. 'Every manager tries to impose his personality on the team, and the smartest thing Gould did was recruit Don Howe, who was the best coach probably in the world at that time,' said Downes. 'Don has seen us play extensively and very early on told Gould not to change anything and it was a massive boost to us to be verified in this way. Obviously Don worked with us individually and kept everything very tight, but focused on continuing the progress.'

Another home victory over Manchester United and a 3-1 drubbing of Arsenal were the highlights at Plough Lane. The real excitement began in January 1988 and the third round of the FA Cup. Wimbledon's journey began at Plough Lane against West Bromwich Albion as the Dons despatched them 4-1 and moved into round four. Wins over Mansfield Town, Newcastle United and Watford meant that Wimbledon had reached the semi-final of this famous old competition, where a hard-working Luton Town side faced them at White Hart Lane. Luton had already beaten Arsenal in the League Cup Final just a few weeks earlier and were clearly in the mood for another Wembley visit. Mick Harford notched for the Hatters but Wimbledon marched through to the final with goals from John Fashanu and Dennis Wise.

And so to Wembley for the FA Cup Final. All schoolboys dream of walking out on that pitch on a boiling hot Saturday in May. Dave Beasant, Clive Goodyear, Terry Phelan, Eric Young, Andy Thorn, Alan Cork, Vinnie Jones, Lawrie Sanchez, Dennis Wise, John Fashanu and Terry Gibson had that chance for Wimbledon. What stood in their way was a Liverpool team who had romped to the First Division title, nine points ahead of Alex Ferguson's Manchester United in second place. Liverpool were attempting to become the first side in English football to win the double for a second time. The Reds from Merseyside were huge favourites. The Dons from Wimbledon were written off even before a ball was kicked.

Wimbledon had been written off on entering the Football League, then on gaining promotion to the Third Division, the Second, and again on reaching the First Division. The club, and most importantly the players, thrived on this kind of attitude. Dublin's *Evening Herald* published the headline 'Liverpool's polish and sophistication will be matched against the blood and thunder football of Wimbledon on FA Cup final day' on the eve of the match. Meanwhile, an article in the *Aberdeen Evening Express* said, 'Wembley is bracing itself for the biggest culture clash in its history and no one should take the result of the 107th FA Cup Final for granted. The bookies may not see anything stopping elegant Liverpool becoming the first club to complete a second league and cup double at Wembley today. But street-wise Wimbledon have never respected tradition, reputation or the form book.'

The game kicked off and within seconds Jones's monstrous tackle on opposing number Steve McMahon had set the tone. Liverpool were looking dangerous and were unlucky not to take the lead midway through the first half when John Barnes and Ronnie Whelan were both thwarted by Beasant. Then came the moment of glory. In the 37th minute, Phelan's run down the left touchline was adjudged to have been impeded by the referee. Wise placed the ball down by the corner flag and whipped in an absolute peach of a cross. The ball arced beautifully towards the corner of the six-yard box where Sanchez rose to glance his header into the far corner of Bruce Grobbelaar's net.

Liverpool piled forward in the second half and Wimbledon were more than holding their own until John Aldridge was brought down by Goodyear just inside the box. The referee pointed to the spot but it was viewed as a harsh decision, Liverpool were usually successful from the spot around that time. Aldridge dusted himself down and stroked the ball to Beasant's left. Fortunately for Wimbledon, Beasant had anticipated this and saved well, also becoming the first goalkeeper to save a penalty in a final. As the minutes ticked by, so did the nerves on the Wimbledon bench. Gould removed his jacket as the pressure and humidity grew. A last throw of the dice for Liverpool was a long throw into the area, but Steve Nicol's bullet header sailed agonisingly over the crossbar. It was agonising for Liverpool anyway. The boys in blue breathed a huge sigh of relief as Beasant placed the ball on the edge of the six-yard box for the restart.

The referee eventually blew the full-time whistle and the Wimbledon players dropped to their knees. They had done it. Utopia. To make things even sweeter, Dave Bassett was in the stands to see his boys crowned cup winners.

Gould had guided the Dons to glory that season but it was a foundation built on Bassett's team. A club that ten years previously were turning out in the depths of non-league football had masterminded a rise through four divisions and upset the footballing world with a knockout blow to the First Division champions. They were a team who fought harder than any other, on a shoestring budget.

Players would ask Bassett for an extra fiver a week and have to flick a coin for the outcome. They were a Sunday league outfit with a professionalism like no other. Yes, they cut their cloth accordingly, and yes it didn't always fit the stereotype but it was successful. Rumours of Bassett using the stadium's CCTV footage on Mondays to go over set pieces and goals scored and conceded are both beautiful and pragmatic.

This fairytale will never be repeated in my lifetime. The money has crept into the game now and even in League One and Two you can be talking telephone numbers to sign players. Wimbledon FC no longer exists in its original form. But they were a treat. Batsford, Bassett and Gould all had a part to play in that magical rise.

8

AC Milan
Sacchi and Capello

Catenaccio
noun: a very defensive system of play,
especially one employing a sweeper. Italian
word for door bolt

WE HEAD to Italy now where quite arguably one of the greatest club teams in the history of football was formed.

Although it is hard to debate the actual greatest and your argument is always going to be subjective, but for a period between 2008 and 2012, Barcelona were absolutely fantastic both domestically and on the European scene. Pep Guardiola's Catalonian giants were nigh-on unbeatable over the course of that four-year period, although a volcanic ash cloud ambushed the team's ambitions during the 2009/10 Champions League campaign.

If Iceland's most active volcano hadn't decided to make a show of itself in 2010, I genuinely believe that Barcelona would have claimed a hat-trick of Champions League titles, given that they had already beaten Manchester United in the 2009 final and would do the same again in 2011, sandwiched either side of this natural disaster. Barcelona were on course for another successful jaunt and had dispatched Arsenal 6-3 on aggregate in the 2010 quarter-final stage and were surely going to send José Mourinho's Inter Milan side packing too. The volcanic dust cloud meant that air travel was impossible and with UEFA not budging on re-arranging the fixture, Barcelona headed to the San Siro by road. It was to be a monster journey of around 12 hours by coach. Inter won the first leg 3-1 and Barcelona never really recovered in the second leg despite winning 1-0.

Another honourable mention to the greatest club sides would have to be Manchester United. Their 1999 treble side did it all over a course of a season and their own version of the 2008–2012 team nearly rivalled Guardiola's Barca. Unfortunately for United, the defeats to Barcelona meant that they would play bridesmaid in this tale. Three Premier League trophies in a row as well as three Champions League finals in four seasons enables them to creep into people's thinking, but ultimately they just fall short.

For fans of an older persuasion, and a more romantic outing, AC Milan from the mid-1980s to mid-'90s, are up there as one of the absolute best. There's something quite magical about the names mentioned in this team, but we will get on to that in a moment. Firstly we need to meet the man who moulded these players into not just a winning team, but also an entertaining unit.

Arrigo Sacchi was a shoe salesman in his native Italy. His playing career never took in any professional clubs but that didn't stop Sacchi from dreaming of making it to the big time. He would study meticulously the football played by the famous Holland team of the 1970s, coached by the well-respected Rinus Michels. A student of the game, the Italian would love the way that this beautiful, orange Dutch unit would surge forward playing such flamboyant football. Rattling around in the lower leagues of Italian football, Sacchi was just waiting for his big chance and Fiorentina gave the scarpa pusher the opportunity he desired. Florence would coax the coach into its city and Sacchi would flourish in Tuscany, taking charge of the youth team.

When things are going well in football, good words spread fast. Sacchi was quickly gaining a reputation as a coach and it wasn't too long before Parma, then in Serie C1, came knocking. Half a decade of schooling himself prior to this had led him to this moment. In 1985, Sacchi would puff out his chest and stroll into the Parma dressing room, demanding that he be respected. In his first full season as the manager, Sacchi led Parma to C1 promotion. He didn't stop there and Parma marched through Serie B in the next campaign, playing a brand of football that was unorthodox in Italy at that time. Disappointingly for Sacchi and the team, they missed out on promotion to Serie A by three points. Despite this, a highlight of the season was the victory over Milan in the Coppa Italia. Again, when things are going well, people seem to sit up and take notice.

Silvio Berlusconi had clearly taken notice, seeing as his Milan team had been humbled by the lower-league side right before his very eyes. The wealthy owner, who had only a year previously taken over the Milanese club and saved them from bankruptcy, was hungry for success. Milan had not won a title in over ten seasons, unless you include Serie B three years previously after a disastrous relegation at the turn of the decade. Milan had been relegated in 1980 after a match-fixing scandal accused them of wrongdoing. They bounced back to Serie A immediately but were unable to retain their top-tier status after their finances had fallen into a state of turmoil. A second Serie B title in three seasons meant that Milan were again back among Italy's big boys, although feeling a little like a plus one at a wedding. Berlusconi could sense that with a little direction, Milan could once again become a powerhouse to be feared.

With Nils Lindholm being moved out of the manager's seat, Berlusconi had decisions to make. Fabio Capello, a coach brought in from Primavera, steadied the ship until the end of the 1986/87 campaign. Capello himself was forging a decent career and was making a real case for the job on a permanent basis, but it was Sacchi who Berlusconi wanted to realise his dream. As the season drew close, Berlusconi made his move and appointed Sacchi, who would make his way from Florence to Milan. The press were slightly stumped and many mocked the appointment. Sacchi was not fazed by the criticism and fired back with, 'I never realised that in order to become a jockey you have to have been a horse first.'

Milan had yo-yoed between Serie A and B during the first half of the 1980s, during which time Juventus won four titles in a six-year spell. Even Roma and little

Hellas Verona had tasted championship champagne while Milan were simply just trying to get their own house in order. Berlusconi had plans. Juventus had won their titles by playing the famed Italian *Catenaccio* style, which was based on defending first, then attacking with caution. The door-bolt back line would soak up opposition attacks and then break at them when possession was lost. Berlusconi was not interested in this at all. If he was going to plough millions of lire into a football club, then the least they could do is entertain him. Sacchi was seen as the man to bring this brand of football to the new owner. Capello need not have worried though as his place was to be alongside Sacchi in the role of assistant.

The team was already sprinkled with stardust. Franco Baresi, Roberto Donadoni and an up-and-coming young defender by the name of Paolo Maldini were considered the outstanding performers. Sacchi knew that with a few more additions, the likes of Juventus and Roma wouldn't be so far out of reach. He raided the latter team and Carlo Ancelotti, a central midfielder and captain of the capital city club, made his way to Milan. Piecing together the jigsaw had begun. The team was very Italian in style and Milan had some high quality players, so they headed to Holland to help provide the verve and flair. Ruud Gullit and Marco van Basten were brought in and slotted in beautifully. Sacchi had always admired the Dutch sides when growing up and was looking for a touch of foreign sauce to add to the mix. Gullit was ripping it up as a playmaker and van Basten's record for Ajax of 128 league goals in 133 appearances led to Sacchi prising open Berlusconi's cheque book for the pair.

Napoli boasted the talents of Diego Maradona and Careca so Sacchi knew it was going to be a tall order, and the 1987/88 season would be the toughest test in his managerial career so far. His 4-4-2 formation would stump some teams with many still playing a sweeper in a five-man defence or a flat back four. Sacchi's philosophy was to pin the opposition back in areas that they were not comfortable playing in and then attempt to outnumber them all over the pitch. His team were extremely hard-working but also very talented. A victory over Juventus and a double against fancied Napoli meant that people were sitting up to take notice of Milan. Goals were being scored by Gullit, who was playing as either a floating second striker or an attacking midfielder. Teams were unsure of how to pick up the Dutchman with Gullit drifting into pockets between defence and midfield. The main goal threat with the team playing alongside the young van Basten was Pietro Paolo Virdis.

Serie A only boasted 16 teams at that time and was still operating with two points for a win. Milan took advantage of the draw only leading to one dropped point and claimed 11 of them. This was coupled with 17 wins, enough to see them home and dry as Scudetto winners. Sacchi's team only lost twice in his opening season, at home to both Fiorentina and Roma. In the 30 games played, Milan only conceded 14 goals. The three-point gap over a Maradona-inspired Napoli ensured that Milan would start the 1988/89 season in the European Cup, something that not even Berlusconi could have imagined happening so quickly.

Virdis had led the line for Milan for nearly a decade but with the 21-year-old van Basten having signed a year previously, Virdis, despite scoring 13 times in the title season, would see his game time begin to diminish. Van Basten had struggled to adapt at first to his new surroundings but when a third Dutchman arrived, van Basten started to feel more at home. Frank Rijkaard was signed to add to the midfield unit and create a Dutch triumvirate. Rijkaard had begun his career as a tough-tackling centre-back. Sacchi saw that he could also play a bit and moved him into the middle of the pitch to act as the ball winner. With van Basten now being trusted to lead the front line, Gullit was the link-up man between him and the midfield. It was a tactic that bamboozled opposition and brought a period of success that even Sacchi may not have dreamt of. The 1988/89 campaign was another entanglement with Napoli. Maradona was god-like down in Naples and having just missed out on the title the year before, he was desperate not to be the bridesmaid this time around. Milan seemingly took their eyes off the prize domestically with a third-place finish and Napoli's double over them cemented the title, although Sacchi's men were focussing their attention elsewhere.

Sampdoria claimed the Coppa Italia and faced Milan in the Supercoppa Italiana but Sacchi's side were victorious with a 3-1 triumph thanks to goals from Rijkaard, van Basten and Mannari. The European Cup had also captured the imagination at the San Siro. Sacchi had taken his team on a European tour that included the likes of Bulgaria, Yugoslavia, Germany and Spain. Levski Sofia were dispatched 7-2 on aggregate in the first round and then a penalty shoot-out victory over Red Star Belgrade extended their run. Werder Bremen were next on the hit-list and were stern opposition but Milan went through 1-0. The semi-final on the other hand would be an altogether different story. Real Madrid lay in wait and while this may have been a mouth-watering tie in the past, with Milan still finding their way back, many doubted that their progression in the tournament would continue. The first leg at the Bernabéu was a tight affair and a 1-1 draw in the Spanish capital suggested that with the home leg to play, Milan were far from out of the tie. Back at the San Siro, the brilliance of Sacchi's team destroyed the aristocrats of European club football as the Rossoneri subjected the Spanish champions to a 5-0 hammering.

A Madrid side consisting of the likes of Manolo Sanchis, Michel, Bernd Schuster, Emiliano Butragueno and Hugo Sanchez was put to the sword by Sacchi's swashbuckling Milan. Goals by Ancelotti, Rijkaard, Gullit, van Basten and Donadoni swept the Rossoneri into the European Cup Final with the pick of the goals being when Donadoni took off down the wing, drove his way past his opponent and crossed for Gullit to power his header home. 'The old men of Real Madrid last night disintegrated,' wrote David Miller in *The Times*. 'They fell apart against the scintillating football of Rijkaard, Donadoni, Ancelotti, Van Basten and Gullit, and Milan galloped into the European Cup final to the delight of a 75,000 crowd.' Van Basten said in his autobiography, 'It was a great feeling to be part of such a strong team that could put the opponent in such a corner... Of course, the Sacchi system was strong, but ultimately the quality of the players was decisive. That victory over

Real in a delirious San Siro had brought us to Barcelona in this final.'

Sacchi knew that just reaching the final itself would not be enough to appease the enigmatic owner who had backed him so trustingly. Steaua Bucharest were waiting for Milan in the Nou Camp, as were over 97,000 punters, eager to see if the Italian top brass could see off a Gheorge Hagi-inspired Romanian outfit. Bucharest were no mugs and also included a young Dan Petrescu plus the lively forward Marius Lacatus. Bucharest had won the trophy just three seasons previously, so to think this was going to be a rollover for Milan would be foolish.

But the final would indeed become another demolition job. Galli kept goal, while Tassotti, Maldini, Baresi and Costacurta patrolled the back line. In front of them roamed a midfield of Colombo, Donadoni, Ancelotti and Pinato. Leading the line was the prolific van Basten while tucked in just behind was the imperious Gullit. Three goals in a scintillating first half enabled Milan to head into half-time with a bit of breathing space. A brace each from Gullit and van Basten enabled Milan to complete their climb from the obscurity and embarrassment of the 1980 match-fixing scandal to the dizzy heights of becoming crowned champions of Europe.

Sacchi had led this team of Italian pragmatism and Dutch wizardry into the upper echelons of world football. Marco the magnificent finished the campaign on an impressive 32 goals and was the darling of the San Siro, but he didn't rest on his laurels in 1989/90 by again breaching the 20-goal mark as Milan plundered more silverware. A hat-trick of cup competitions was claimed but Sacchi's side again fell short in Serie A, finishing runners-up to a Gianluca Vialli-inspired Sampdoria. His attentions again though were drawn to the European scene.

First up was a 2-1 European Super Cup victory over UEFA Cup holders Barcelona. A 1-1 draw in the first leg in Spain set up a finely poised second leg in which Milan stumbled over the line at the San Siro for a 1-0 win, van Basten again flexing his finishing muscle. Next up was a trip to Tokyo where over 60,000 fans crammed into the national stadium where Milan saw off Colombia's Atlético Nacional 1-0 to win the Intercontinental Cup. A goal in the last seconds of extra time was enough to claim the crown of the season, Alberico Evani scoring it and also claiming the man of the match champagne for his troubles.

The European Cup campaign was also in full flow. This time en route to the final in Vienna, Milan dispatched HJK Helsinki 5-0 on aggregate in the first round before being matched in a second-round tie against Real Madrid, their opponents in the previous season's semi-final. It is said that this match was symbolic of how the European Cup is now played in its current format, the Champions League. Berlusconi made noises about the tie, complaining that one of the big hitters would be crashing out so early in the competition. It was around this time, and with the help of Berlusconi and a crack task force from other top clubs, that a committee was formed to lobby for a super league-style trophy. Fast forward a few seasons and voila, the birth of the Champions League.

Milan again put Madrid to the sword at the San Siro, finishing with a two-goal lead. Madrid pulled one back at the Bernabéu but it wasn't enough to overturn that first-leg deficit. Mechelen would provide a stern test but after a 0-0 draw in the Belgian city, it took an extra-time double at the San Siro to book another semi-final berth, this time against another European powerhouse in the shape of Bayern Munich. Milan squeezed home 1-0 in the first leg and must have thought they had done enough to see the tie through when they travelled to Munich. Bayern had other ideas and managed to notch to send the match to extra time again. But Milan were now masters of playing through the 90-minute mark and again showed their mettle to advance to the final despite losing 2-1 on the night, the away goals rule saving the bacon of Sacchi and his men.

The capital of Austria hosted the final in 1990 and Sacchi only made one change from the team that had romped to victory the year previously. Evani, who had been playing magnificently, pipped Pinato to the left-midfield spot. Benfica boasted a squad with Portuguese Brazilian players, and even a Swede. Sacchi, though, knew that on their day, his team would put away any side in front of them. This again would be their day as a Frank Rijkaard goal midway through the second half meant that Milan became the first team to retain the trophy since Nottingham Forest in 1980.

In the three seasons that Sacchi had taken control of the Rossoneri, Sacchi had guided them to a Serie A title and runner-up position domestically as well as a Supercoppa win, plus twin European Cup glories as well as the

Intercontinental Cup and Super Cup. The Italian FA, fresh from the national team's third-place finish in Italia '90, was keen on what was happening in Milan. Rumours were rife that Sacchi could be the man to replace the outward-heading Azeglio Vacini. Did Sacchi have his head turned? Coaching your national team would surely be the pinnacle in anyone's career. Milan will never know if that was the case and only Sacchi could say.

A season of better the devil you know followed with Milan again claiming European Super Cup and Intercontinental Cup success. Fellow Italian club Sampdoria were beaten 3-1 on aggregate in the Super Cup while another trip to Tokyo again bore fruit when Paraguayans Olimpia were soundly beaten 3-0 in the national stadium. Van Basten himself had a stop-start season in 1990/91 and with injuries holding him back, Milan again finished as runners-up in Serie A. The European Cup, which had for over two years brought unbridled success, would this time become a trip hazard on Milan's quest to claim a hat-trick of trophies.

The run to the final seemed to be going smoothly. A first-round bye was followed by a second-round victory over Club Brugge, 1-0 on aggregate. But a quarter-final meeting with French club Marseille would have severe consequences. After a 1-1 draw in the first leg in Milan, Sacchi took his team to the south of France and plotted a smash-and-grab raid. Chris Waddle notched for Marseille and with the game ticking into added time, the hosts were certain to go through. Then came the controversy as half of the floodlights at the Stade Velodrome went out. With half the pitch plunged into darkness, the referee had no alternative but to take both teams back to the dressing rooms. Milan's sporting director Adriano Galliani was incensed and was absolutely sure that the French had manufactured the malfunction. It was around 20 minutes before the light was restored and with Galliani still furious, he refused to send his team back on to the field. UEFA awarded Marseille a 3-0 forfeit win and with worse news to follow, Milan and Galliani were subsequently banned from all European competitions the following campaign. It was a tough pill for Sacchi to swallow after all his outstanding work.

The season closed out and in the summer of 1991, Sacchi was ultimately appointed as the manager of Italy. The side-note to this impressive story is that in the next World Cup in USA, 1994, a Milan-loaded side played the same 4-4-2 system. Despite losing their first match to the Republic of Ireland, Sacchi led this unfancied team all the way to the final and they were unlucky to lose on a penalty shoot-out against Brazil. His defensive general Baresi missed his kick, as did Ballon d'Or winner Roberto Baggio.

Berlusconi was a clever man. When appointing Fabio Capello a few seasons previously to steady the ship before eventually choosing Sacchi, Berlusconi had wanted to keep the up-and-coming coach around. With Sacchi making Capello his deputy, it was a seamless move for Berlusconi to slot Capello straight into the vacant hotseat. Who better than someone who knew the plan, the players and the ideology of the owner? The media were circling as Milan had crashed out of the quarter-final stage of the European Cup and finished runners-up in the league. Ageing players in Baresi, Ancelotti and Tassotti, were pinpointed as a weakness for the Rossoneri but Capello was smart. He knew that these players were the backbone of this side and informed them of that. Different manager, same system.

With no European football to contend with in 1991/92, Milan had only domestic matters to concentrate on. Serie A had often been a distraction when in fact it should have been the team's bread and butter. Capello enforced his ideas on to the squad but changed very little in both personnel and tactics. He certainly didn't try and re-invent the wheel but simply tweaked it slightly to suit his players. What followed was a sheer dominance on the pitch that no club in Italy could deal with. Milan dispatched Roma, Napoli and Sampdoria, 4-1, 5-0 and 5-1 respectively. Capello's Milan were flying and van Basten again netted over 25 goals as they cruised to Serie A glory. In his first full season as manager, Capello, like Sacchi before him, had led the Rossoneri to the Scudetto.

The glorious cherry on this fantastic cake was that Milan had also gone the entire season without tasting defeat. Just when Capello's men looked to relinquish their record in the final game of the season, they showed the kind of character that Capello and Sacchi would be proud of. Trailing 2-1 away to Foggia, Milan roared back to hit them for eight and finish the season with a flourish. Of their 34 matches they had won 22 and drawn 12, conceding only 21 goals. European qualification had again been achieved and with Milan's ban now complete, Capello could lead his side into a continental battle the following season.

What Capello didn't know was that 1991/92 would be the last full season that van Basten would complete, with an ankle injury curtailing his career far too soon at the age of 31. Van Basten, who had won his third Ballon d'Or in 1992, eventually retired in 1995 but hadn't kicked a ball for nearly two seasons. Capello, noticing that van Basten was not firing on all cylinders, brought in Marseille's Jean-Pierre Papin, who had won the top honour himself in 1991.

Worry not Fabio. Milan again swept all before them domestically, firstly claiming the Supercoppa Italia naand then marching towards another Scudetto. They again blew teams away with their goalscoring prowess with both Papin and van Basten finishing with 20 goals each. Victories over Napoli, Fiorentina and Sampdoria were the highlights of another successful campaign. Continuing from the previous season's unbeaten run, Milan stretched their invincible record to 58 games before defeat to Juventus ended their magical period of dominance. It certainly didn't knock Capello's men off their stride as again they were the champions of Italy.

The European Cup had been quite kind to Milan during Sacchi's reign. Capello had witnessed first-hand the excitement of competition and wanted to taste a piece of the action for himself. Milan had missed out on the inaugural campaign for the new and glitzy Champions League due to suspension, but this time they were among the team contending for the title. The previous system of straight knockout rounds had been altered with a couple of early rounds followed by two groups of four, with the group winners going through to the final. The new group stage format was added for extra spice, and revenue of course. Milan put away Ljubljana of Slovenia in round one and then Slovan Bratislava of the Czech Republic in round two. Group stage opponents were also put to the sword in the shape of Porto, IFK Gothenburg and PSV Eindhoven. Milan topped the group with 12 points from 18 and headed through to the final.

Marseille, Milan's nemesis from Sacchi's final season, had topped their group and were waiting for Capello in Munich. With revenge on the cards, Capello set about a game plan to stump the French outfit. Massaro was brought in to partner van Basten, which was a slight surprise considering Papin's goal record that season. Marseille, though, were no small fry and with players such as Alen Boksic, Marcel Desailly, Basile Boli, Didier Deschamps and Rudi Voller, it was clear that the French team were again looking to do a number on the Italians. Marseille played a 3-5-2 system which clogged up the midfield. Capello stuck with his traditional 4-4-2 but could not find a way out of the suffocation. On the stroke of half-time, Boli scored for Marseille and Milan never really recovered, although Capello was bruised but not beaten. The French team lifted old big ears and again foiled the Rossoneri.

Sometimes in football you learn more in defeat than in victory and Capello arrived in the pre-season of 1993/94 in bullish mood. The team were still smarting from that defeat to Marseille and began the season in winning form. A trip to Washinton DC for the Supercoppa Italiana was on the cards. Different venue, same outcome, and Milan beat Torino 1-0 to claim the trophy for the second year running. With the injury to van Basten limiting his minutes, Milan's goal threat had nearly vanished. Big wins were a thing of the past as consistency and efficiency were the order of the day, and this season would see no games won by more than a two-goal margin. The defence was as tight as usual but the attack was finding goals hard to come by and Daniele Massaro, leading the line, scored just 16.

Defeats in both the Intercontinental Cup and Super Cup – Milan played in the latter despite losing the Champions League Final as Marseille were subsequently banned for match-fixing – had Capello wondering if his squad were maybe too over-reliant on the brilliance of van Basten. Luckily for Capello, the doubters were proved wrong and with a third successive Serie A title claimed, they breathed a huge sigh of relief. Despite winning a hat-trick of domestic titles, Milan saved their absolute best for Europe once again.

Milan started like a train and romped past FC Aurau and Copenhagen in the first and second round respectively. The group stages were much tougher this time around though and with goals being hard to come by, Milan somehow managed to scrape through to the final with a hard-fought ten points from a possible 18. The group contained Werder Bremen, Porto and Anderlecht. Milan went undefeated but only won two games and drew the rest. Luckily enough it was better than the other teams could achieve and Milan were in a second successive final.

Capello had been caught out by a well-rehearsed Marseille side a year previously and he was in no mood for a repeat performance. The problem facing Milan was that they were to take on Johan Cruyff's swashbuckling Barcelona team. Barca were made clear favourites with their imperious style of football but Capello played up to the underdog tag. Cruyff boasted the likes of Romario, Hristo Stoichkov, Ronald Koeman and Pep Guardiola. Capello had bolstered his midfield with the energetic Marcel Desailly, who had impressed the coach with his performance for Marseille in the previous final.

Massaro, who had taken some stick for not being van Basten, struck midway through the first half and just as Barcelona were beginning to find their feet, he scored again in stoppage time. This made Capello's team talk simpler as his team were not known to throw away goals. In fact, in the 196 matches that Paolo Maldini partnered Franco Baresi in central defence for Milan, only 23 goals were conceded. It was an absolutely fantastic record and included this final as Barcelona could not find a way through. Dejan Savicevic scored in the 47th minute to put the game to bed and to add to the performance, Desailly capped off a magnificent display with the fourth just before the hour.

Capello had matched his predecessor and claimed a Champions League win. Like Sacchi before him, Capello had continued the style which Berlusconi had dreamt of when he saved the club from going to the wall. Milan had spent the last part of the decade dominating on both the domestic and European front. The Rossoneri played an attacking 4-4-2 under Sacchi that teams just couldn't deal with. Once the goal threat of van Basten had begun to dry up, Capello decided to play a more pragmatic style, but still utilising the same system. Ultimately for Milan, it bore huge success.

Grazie, Arrigo and Fabio.

9

Leicester City
Trip to Wonderland

Wonderland
noun: a land or place full of
wonderful things

RICHARD III was buried in Leicester, which ironically was the same fate as the other 19 Premier League clubs metaphorically suffered during the 2015/16 campaign. Over the course of that special season, Leicester City were to be the cream of the crop and after odds of around 5,000/1 to win the title before the campaign started, this was considered one of the most incredible sporting underdog stories in history. Leicester had never won the top league during their 130-year existence until 'the most unlikely triumph in the history of team sport', as described by the BBC Sport website.

The path to that glory began with heartbreak three years previously. Deep into stoppage time in the second

AN ODE TO FOUR FOUR TWO

leg of their play-off semi-final at Watford, Anthony Knockaert was stood waiting for the referee to blow his whistle. Watford were leading Leicester 2-1 on the day but the game was tied at 2-2 on aggregate. Leicester, however, had been awarded a very late penalty and were one kick away from the final.

With the ball on the penalty spot, Knockaert took a deep breath before starting his run-up. The left-footed forward struck the ball low to Manuel Almunia's left-hand side, only to see the Watford stopper go the same way. Almunia blocked the penalty but Knockaert was on to the rebound as quick as a flash. The Frenchman slammed the ball towards the goal but somehow Almunia had managed to get up and block the shot, showing amazing reflexes.

Watford managed to scramble the ball clear and it found its way up to Fernando Forestieri, who drove down the right-hand channel. He beat his man and stood up a delicious cross to the back post. Hogg, unmarked, unselfishly headed the ball back across goal to Watford's talisman Troy Deeney. From seven yards out, Deeney rifled home to end Leicester's promotion dream and send Watford to Wembley. Knockaert was spread out on the turf in tears and anyone else associated with the club was dumbstruck. From the brink of a trip to the play-off final to heartbreak in 15 short seconds was a cruel, cruel end to a season.

Nigel Pearson would have his work cut out to pick this squad up off its knees. 'Anthony is distraught as you would expect,' admitted City manager Pearson in his post-match press conference. 'I'm the first to admit it was a generous penalty decision. But to concede off the resulting penalty save is very hard to take. Unfortunately that's the nature of the beast. It can be a very cruel game at times and for the players to experience that is very tough.' With heartbreak still fresh in the minds of the squad, the players were sent on their summer breaks with one instruction: to enjoy the break because they would be working hard to rectify the defeat on their return.

The beginning of the 2013/14 campaign was to be a good yardstick with only one defeat coming in the August. The squad was kept together and the tight-knit atmosphere in the group was starting to show. Wins over Wigan, Blackburn and Barnsley ensured an unbeaten September and Leicester were starting to look in good nick. All was looking rosy in the garden until two defeats on the spin threatened to derail the Foxes' promotion charge as the winter months began to draw in. Away defeats to Sheffield Wednesday and Brighton, 2-1 and 3-1 respectively, during the first week of December, looked to dent the push for Premier League football.

The team headed to Loftus Road on 21 December to face a very talented Queens Park Rangers team, managed by Harry Redknapp. With the recent wobble fresh in the memory, Pearson sent out the side he thought could turn the tide against Rangers and re-ignite Leicester's promotion push. The starting 11 that afternoon was Kasper Schmeichel in goal, Ritchie De Laet and Paul Konchesky at full-back, Liam Moore and Wes Morgan in the centre of defence, Lloyd Dyer and Knockaert on the wings, Matty James and Danny Drinkwater holding the centre of the park, and Jamie Vardy up front alongside David Nugent.

QPR included ex-England goalkeeper Rob Green as well as the likes of Richard Dunne, Clint Hill, Joey Barton, Yossi Benayoun, Jermaine Jenas, the sharp-shooting Charlie Austin, and the Croatian maverick Niko Kranjcar.

The hosts dominated. QPR bossed possession and had a whole host of chances but were unable to capitalise, largely due to both poor finishing and the fine form of Schmeichel. Leicester sensed that this could be their day. When Drinkwater's pass was flicked on by Nugent, Vardy raced on and fired low beyond the helpless Green. It was cool, calm and ruthless by the forward, and very much a trademark move of the team. The Foxes held on for a 1-0 victory despite a barrage of attacks from the home side. 'It was always going to be important to get something out of the game today, so to get away from here with three points is a very good return,' said Pearson, talking to the BBC. 'They are a good side. I felt we created good opportunities, but they will probably feel they should have got something out of the game, especially after the first-half situations they had. We are delighted. We've only scored one goal again, but the key is that we've actually kept a clean sheet and we've not kept enough of those this season.'

Sensing that the team needed a pick-me-up, Pearson strengthened his squad in the January with the signing of Riyad Mahrez from Le Havre, for an undisclosed fee. This was just the timely boost that the squad needed. Mahrez was inspirational in the run-in. The unknown Algerian from the lower leagues in France lit up Leicester's performances. Despite a slight wobble when losing away at Brighton on 7 December, Leicester would not taste defeat again until 8

April, a run that saw them win 15 times from 20 attempts. When Pearson's men defeated QPR at the tail-end of April, the Premier League was in touching distance.

Nugent and Vardy had blown away opposition defences and scored nearly 40 goals between them in a devastating partnership, which epitomised why the Foxes had made Vardy the first £1m player signed from non-league football. His pace and keen eye for a finish was proving too much for Championship defenders, showing that Leicester were right to risk bringing him in from Fleetwood Town. Nugent was no mug himself. Having played the majority of his career between both Championship and Premier League, he knew his way around the opposition's box and was certainly a great foil for the more direct Vardy.

Leicester's 1-0 win at Bolton Wanderers sealed the deal on 22 April, elevating the Foxes into the top tier of English football once again as champions. In a time when foreign coaches had instilled a different kind of system in England, Leicester and Pearson had stuck with the tried and trusted 4-4-2 formation, the taste of champagne washing away the taste of heartache from the previous year. The hard work didn't stop there as Pearson knew he would need to continue in the same vein when approaching the Premier League. 'I think it's a relief for a lot of people,' said Pearson. 'It's been a tough couple of years in the sense that we've been trying to get back into the top flight and it's never easy.' Schmeichel continued with the same theme, 'It feels great. It's an amazing achievement. We are all very, very happy and it's a great day for everyone at the club. What we wanted all along was promotion.'

The 2014/15 campaign was always going to be about survival. Consolidation is always key before trying to build on the momentum, but that is always easier said than done. Pearson strengthened his squad with experienced free transfers in the shape of Matthew Upson from Brighton, and the Argentinian midfielder Esteban Cambiasso, who was a free agent. Winger Marc Albrighton was also drafted in on a free from Aston Villa while £8m was splashed out on Argentinian striker, Leonardo Ulloa, also from Brighton. Another £2m was spent on full-back Danny Simpson, who would be a great addition having played the year previous at QPR.

The battle plans were drawn up and with new signings beginning to bed in well after pre-season, it was down to the task of maintaining Premier League status, but August brought just two points from a possible nine. September was a lot more promising after wins against Stoke City and Manchester United. The 5-3 victory over United was seen as a seismic effort, especially after the visitors had just shelled out on Bastian Schweinsteiger, Angel Di Maria and Radamel Falcao, and led 3-1 at one stage. It would prove to be a false dawn, however, as the Leicester players wouldn't earn more win bonus money until 28 December.

Rock bottom at Christmas is never ideal in any situation but in the Premier League, only West Bromwich Albion in 2004/05 and Sunderland in 2013/14 had managed to survive the drop. The new year then brought brief respite with wins over Hull City and Aston Villa, and a draw at Anfield had heralded some hope before five defeats in eight games cemented Leicester's position at the foot of the table.

The writing was on the wall for Pearson, who was under an immense amount of pressure, so much so that when James McArthur of Crystal Palace bundled into the boss during the Foxes' 1-0 defeat in the February, Pearson held on to the Palace midfielder while on the floor and refused to let go, leading to a dust-up between the pair.

When asked by the BBC why he held on to the player, Pearson replied, 'Because he said something to me.' When asked to elaborate he simply replied, 'I don't have to reveal anything, do I? I'm more than capable of looking after myself.' McArthur responded by saying, 'I got a bit scared to be honest. These things happen and you see quite a lot of it between players and managers throughout the game.' The manager was clearly up for the scrap and it was time for the players to stand up and be counted. The old saying 'one in, all in' was never more prevalent to this Leicester side than at that point in the season.

Pearson's men were seven points from safety with nine games remaining. It was shit or bust and a home victory over West Ham started the revival. Further wins over Burnley, West Bromwich Albion and Swansea meant that it was a fruitful April, despite losing on the final game of the month to a Chelsea team who were just about to re-unite José Mourinho with the Premier League title. The winds of change had really settled at the King Power Stadium and despite that setback, Leicester finished the run-in with three victories out of four, only conceding once, when they beat QPR 5-1 in the final game. Against the odds, Pearson had dragged his Leicester side, kicking and screaming, into a healthy 14th-place finish. This was considered a very respectable achievement, even more so given that the team were planted at the foot of the table over the festive period.

Kudos to Pearson, and all his players, for digging in and managing to retain their seat at the top table of English football. Digging in though would be Pearson's undoing as off-the-field reports regarding his son made his position untenable. Pearson was told by the board that his working relationship was no longer viable, and he was relieved from his post. It was a bombshell for the squad who had worked with the gaffer through promotion and escape. But football has a funny way of turning a bad situation into a very good one.

The club announced their replacement for Pearson on 13 July 2015 – Claudio Ranieri. The 'Tinkerman', who had previously managed Chelsea back in the early noughties, was given the job amid scepticism from the media. Marcus Christenson from *The Guardian* wrote, 'If Leicester wanted someone nice, they've got him. If they wanted someone to keep them in the Premier League, then they may have gone for the wrong guy.' The hack could well have had a good insight into his prediction as Ranieri's Greece side had recently been humbled by the Faroe Islands.

When quizzed by the *Leicester Mercury*, Ranieri said, 'I made a mistake when I was manager of Greece. I wanted to look because it is a different job at a club to a national team. I had four matches and for each game I trained the players for just three days. That is 12 days of training. What can I do in just 12 days? I had to rebuild a national team in just 12 days. What could I do? I am not a magician.'

This was not ideal preparation with a new season looming for the Foxes. Three new signings had made it through the door at the King Power, having been agreed prior to Pearson's departure. Christian Fuchs was signed on a free from Schalke 04, Robert Huth joined for £3m from Stoke City and Japanese striker Shinji Okazaki was brought in from Mainz for a fee of around £7m. The board had seen a massive upturn in the team's form towards the tail-end of the season and sanctioned the spending to help push Leicester even further up the table and stave off any further threats of relegation.

Staying in the Premier League is big business and with prize money of around £100m for just retaining league status, plus the money generated in final league position and sponsorship deals, it persuades some clubs to gamble on spending money on elaborate signings. Leicester's transfer dealings during the 2014/15 campaign were mainly free transfers, apart from the £8m splashed out on Ulloa. This proved to be good business though as his 16 goals helped massively towards the revival.

Leicester's most impressive deal during the summer of 2015 was the signing of unknown midfielder N'Golo Kante. A fee of around £5m was paid for the petit-looking Frenchman who was picked up from Caen in another coup from the French league, just like Mahrez six months earlier. Recruitment boss Steve Walsh was charged with finding the talent to fit into this team. Walsh had spotted Mahrez and convinced Pearson that he was the missing piece of the puzzle for promotion. Pearson trusted Walsh. Ranieri was yet to get to grips with his new backroom staff but that didn't stop Walsh from bending the Italian's ear regarding Kante. 'Claudio Ranieri was sceptical,' said Walsh. 'Claudio kept saying, "He's not big enough. Why do I want Kante?" I said, "I'm telling you…"' and Walsh wore down the Italian. Gokhan Inler was also signed from Napoli for £3m but the Swiss international arrived under little fanfare.

Departing during the summer and in the early months of the new season were the likes of Matthew Upson, Esteban Cambiasso, Paul Gallagher, Gary Taylor-Fletcher and Anthony Knockaert, who had disappointed in the Premier League when there was such high expectation to dazzle. Upson was heading towards the twilight of his career, as was Cambiasso, who had made a very limited impact on what can be a demanding and physical division. As well as Walsh, Ranieri decided that he would keep Pearson's coach, Craig Shakespeare. This would prove to be a shrewd move as he had wanted to ensure as little disruption to the club as possible. The pre-season results were just like any other and there was nothing out of the ordinary to suggest that something fantastic was afoot. Wins over Lincoln City, Birmingham City, Burton Albion and Rotherham United completed a whirlwind tour of the Midlands and South Yorkshire as opposed to a glitzy expedition to some far-away country.

Sunderland were the first Premier League visitors to the King Power Stadium in 2015/16. August is always a beautiful time with the sun shining down on the immaculate, billiard table-like pitches, new kits and fans fresh from their summer rest. The home supporters didn't have to wait too long at all to begin to bask in the hazy summer's afternoon. Just 11 minutes were on the clock when Jamie Vardy opened his account for the season. Mahrez added two more and Marc Albrighton rounded off the scoring in an impressive opening-day 4-2 win. West Ham were then put to the sword before two draws against Tottenham and Bournemouth ensured a near-perfect start to the new campaign.

Ranieri had already confounded many of his knockers with his surprisingly English approach to the opening month. Italians, famed for playing a more conservative style rather than a bold and direct approach, would usually set up with two holding midfielders and potentially a back three or sweeper. Shakespeare, who had been at Leicester for several seasons, had clearly briefed Ranieri on the workings of the squad and how they had found a system which had contributed to the upturn of results in their bid for safety. With the end-of-season run and 2015/16 opening, the Foxes had extended their unbeaten sequence to 13 matches. The 4-4-2 formation was still in full flow, very un-Italian indeed. Ranieri, who had earned the nickname 'Tinkerman' for his constant changing of line-ups and formations while at Stamford Bridge, was fooling the press further by sticking to what he considered his settled 11.

But Leicester were brought back down to earth with an almighty bang at the end of September as Arsenal ran riot in a 5-2 win at the King Power. An Alexis Sanchez hat-trick inspired the Gunners to victory despite Vardy bagging himself a brace. It had taken to game week seven for Ranieri and his squad to taste defeat. How they bounced back from this, if even at all, would become a barometer for the next 31 matches. The start to the campaign was decent, but things can turn quickly in football. Loss of form and winless runs can easily creep into the frame.

Not to be deterred, Ranieri would stick by his side and continue in the same fashion that he had started the season. His 4-4-2 formation had heralded success over the opening period, apart from the humbling by Arsenal. Ranieri had organised a team which consisted of Schmeichel, Simpson, Fuchs, Morgan and Huth at the back, Kante acting as the midfield sweeper alongside the more creative Drinkwater, Mahrez and Albrighton occupying the wide areas, with Okazaki providing the perfect foil for the direct running of Vardy.

The Japanese forward worked tirelessly to move defenders around to allow space for Vardy to exploit and run in behind. Kante would win the ball around the edge of his own box and play it to Drinkwater who would hit a long diagonal to either Vardy in the channel or Mahrez, who would just cheat by not tracking back. This would catch teams out time and time again. The opposition knew it was coming, but knowing it and stopping it are two completely different things. Ranieri showed trust in his team. They knew their roles and stuck to them beautifully.

Leicester travelled to Norwich City and immediately got back on track with a plucky 2-1 win to kick-start October. 'We responded very well after our defeat against Arsenal,' said Ranieri in his post-match presser. 'We showed good character and it was a good performance. We have 15 points, 25 less than we need to. After we get that, we will see what happens.' The boss clearly had his eyes on the mythical 40-point mark which is generally accepted to secure Premier League safety. Vardy opened the scoring from the spot with Jeffrey Schlupp adding the all-important second. 'Everyone has seen that we don't lack the fight and team spirit,' said Schlupp. 'We can dig deep when we need to. We can adapt to any situation. Jamie Vardy up front terrorises the defenders. He is a pest and always in the defenders' faces.'

Wins over Watford, West Brom, Crystal Palace and Newcastle extended the run. Vardy had also extended his own scoring run by notching in ten consecutive appearances. Manchester United then headed to the King Power for the final game of November, looking to ignite their own campaign under the guidance of Louis van Gaal. Vardy was hoping to score to break the record of ex-United striker Ruud van Nistelrooy, who had scored in ten games in a row. On 24 minutes, Vardy raced into the right-hand channel and slammed the ball across David de Gea, and into the far corner of the net. United rallied but could only salvage a point.

Leicester were heading into the festive period in good nick and the media were now starting to believe that maybe they could not only stay in the division, but push for a European berth. There were still some doubters, who felt that any time soon, Ranieri's men would trip up and stumble back to the lower depths of the division. Swansea City were put to the sword at the Liberty Stadium with Mahrez taking home the match ball after a comfortable 3-0 win. 'We are thinking about ourselves, to take points and make good football,' said Ranieri to the gathering journalists as he tried to board the coach home. 'That is our first goal, to achieve 40 points, to be safe. It was a tough match because Swansea play very good football. We started very well, we scored three goals, and had a minimum other four clear chances and I'm very pleased. Our fans they must dream, but we must stay calm and keep our feet on the ground.'

Then came the point in the season when people thought that this could actually be the fantasy that becomes a reality. Champions Chelsea headed to the King Power but were having a turbulent season trying to retain their title. A partisan crowd welcomed Mourinho's men and Leicester set about the Blues in emphatic fashion, and Vardy and Mahrez were again the main protagonists in an impressive 2-1 win. Now it was about maintaining momentum. A bittersweet trip to Merseyside followed as first a win at Goodison Park was soon to be overshadowed by defeat to Liverpool just a few days later.

As 2016 chimed in, Ranieri was in no mood to party. His team had made it to the halfway point and he knew that there was more to come from his squad. An away win at Spurs was just the tonic to begin the new year, then victories at Stoke and more emphatically at home to Liverpool drove home the confidence that was surging through the squad. Danny Drinkwater was in chipper mood when interviewed post-Liverpool, 'We're staying on the ground but if we carry on the way we are then why not have the belief to win the league? It would go down in history surely.'

Four days after defeating Liverpool 2-0, the Foxes travelled to Manchester City, who had begun to falter under the stewardship of Manuel Pellegrini, despite battling for the title themselves. Again the size of the task in front of Ranieri's men was huge, but they cared little for reputations or expectations. Mahrez and Vardy again ran riot, which was a theme for the season. Time and again Vardy broke through the static City defence only to be denied by Joe Hart. It was not to be the hit-man's day as the limelight was this time shared between Mahrez and two-goal hero Robert Huth. The big German defender slotted home to open the scoring and then rounded off the match with a superb header. City's consolation in a 3-1 reverse didn't come until three minutes from time.

Ranieri was cool and collected in his presser. He said, 'We play without pressure because we don't have to win the league. We must enjoy. This league is so strange and now it is important to think about Arsenal.' But Arsenal would prove to be a bit of a bogey team for the Foxes. Heading to the Emirates, Ranieri was confident that his team could avenge the 5-2 hammering back in the autumn. Vardy scored from the spot on the stroke of half-time but with Danny Simpson collecting his second yellow directly after the break, things began to unravel as Arsenal equalised through Theo Walcott. The team were pinned back for large portions of the second period and must have thought that they had salvaged a point until, deep into injury time, Danny Welbeck struck to sink a plucky Leicester performance.

Ranieri and his squad had managed to navigate their way through a tricky period of fixtures. In front of them now was a run of games that on paper, Leicester should have been taking points from. Football is not played on paper, it is played on grass, but with the teams occupying the lower regions of the table still to play, even the most pessimistic of Foxes supporters would have started to believe. March hosted three wins from four matches with a draw coming at home to West Brom. Dispatched were Watford, Newcastle and Palace. Vardy was still scoring and even if by some miracle, an opposition back line had managed to keep him quiet, up stepped Okazaki, Mahrez or Albrighton. Even Ulloa chipped in with vital goals from the bench when called upon during a hectic Easter period.

The Argentinian rescued a point at the King Power with an injury-time penalty against West Ham. The 2-2 draw symbolised the team's never-say-die spirit, especially after having Vardy dismissed in the 56th minute for a second booking while leading 1-0. West Ham scored two late goals to turn the match on its head and sour the atmosphere inside the stadium, until the drama right at the end. Ulloa showed great composure for a player who had been on the fringes during the course of the campaign and slammed home the resulting spot kick.

'Our performance 11 v 11 and 10 v 11 was fantastic,' said Ranieri after the final whistle. The backs-to-the-wall display underlined that the team had enough grit in their play to tough it out when it really mattered. The top three were not showing any signs of letting up as Spurs were still chipping away and Arsenal were also grinding out wins. Swansea were next to visit the King Power and without the suspended Vardy, Ranieri again turned to his saviour from the previous fixture. Ulloa didn't disappoint and bagged a brace in an emphatic 4-0 victory. Leicester were now on the brink of winning the Premier League and fans who had amazingly backed their heroes at 5,000/1 were twitching at the thought of whether to hold out or cash in.

Leicester travelled to Manchester United on 1 May. Vardy returned to the starting 11 but their colossal captain Wes Morgan brought the Foxes level in a 1-1 draw. A win would have wrapped up the championship at Old Trafford. The following night, Tottenham headed to out-of-sorts Chelsea and led 2-0 in an ill-tempered match. Chelsea, with only pride to play for, and the ability to end Spurs' title tilt, kicked into life and scored twice to level the match. Leicester's players had gathered at Vardy's house on the off-chance that Spurs couldn't grab the win required to continue the championship race. They sat perched on the edge of Vardy's sofa, kicking every ball and shouting at every decision until finally the match was brought to an end and the unbelievable had occurred. Leicester City were champions of the Premier League.

Gary Lineker, host of the BBC's *Match of the Day*, was as shocked as anyone. He said, 'I can't think of anything that surpasses it in sporting history. It is difficult to put over in words. I got emotional. It was hard to breathe. I was a season ticket holder from the age of seven. This is actually impossible.' The plaudits didn't stop there. Alan Shearer, a Premier League winner with Blackburn Rovers in 1995, said, 'It's the biggest thing ever in football.' Ranieri said, 'I am very happy to win because when you start as a manager you hope you can win a league. I won the most important league in Europe, I think, not just Europe but the world!'

The direct style that Leicester approached each game with was a throwback to times gone by, but it was made effective by the personnel available to Ranieri. Vardy's tireless running and Okazaki's guile were the undoing of most defences. N'Golo Kante proved to be a superb signing. Steve Walsh once joked, 'We play three in midfield; Drinky in the middle and Kanté on either side.' This comment showed just how much work Kante would get through to enable the more creative players to flourish. That's not to say that Kante wasn't a superb footballer in his own right.

With Andrea Bocelli's performance of 'Nessun Dorma' playing out to the King Power Stadium, Leicester City brought down the curtain on their fairytale season with Vardy again showing that he was the business as the Foxes cruised to a 3-1 victory over Everton. In February 2004, Adidas released a campaign titled 'Impossible is Nothing'. Just a few short months later, Greece, who had only twice qualified for a major tournament, shocked the world and defeated Portugal in the European Championship Final. The odds on Leicester lifting the Premier League title were longer that year than Elvis Presley being found alive (3,000/1) and the Loch Ness Monster being spotted (500/1). In a season when the Foxes had only tasted defeat three times, like Greece before them, Leicester showed the world that in fact impossible is nothing.

10

Leeds United
Rampant Revie, Revived by Howard's Way

Revive
verb: restore to life or consciousness

'I AM a firm believer that if you score one goal, the other team have to score two to win.' Pearls of wisdom from manager Howard Wilkinson, a proud Yorkshireman who was known for his black and white approach to football. And it was to be in his native Yorkshire that Wilkinson would shine in the dugout.

The now chairman of the League Managers' Association (LMA) was way ahead of the pack when it came to management. Wilkinson, when quizzed about coaching, once replied, 'Now, if I'm asked my advice by would-be coaches, one of the things I ask them is, "Are you brave enough to be different?" Authenticity, respect, trust. It spells ART which is nice but I think they are really key. If you're not brave enough to be yourself, it's not going to work.' Wilkinson was certainly brave. His decision to move up the M1 to Leeds United from Sheffield Wednesday in October 1988 was considered something of a shock.

Leeds were struggling towards the bottom of the Second Division under the stewardship of club legend Billy Bremner. Wilkinson's Owls, meanwhile, were well established as a First Division side. Wilkinson had taken the job at Hillsborough in 1983 following a fine spell in charge at First Division Notts County. Being ahead of his counterparts was what Wilkinson thrived on. He cut his cloth accordingly at all his clubs and made sure that every ounce of information that was given to him, was utilised.

Wilkinson's Notts County side was famed for its passing style, orchestrated by Scotland's Don Masson in midfield and with Pedro Richards making the switch from a right-back to a sweeper. 'I learned a lot of it from basketball,' said Wilkinson during a chat with the press. 'Full-backs would go wide and push on, centre-backs would split, Masson would drop for possession and the goalkeeper had to throw it. We played Bristol City in a friendly and they had a well-known midfielder playing, and we are walking off and he said, "Play like that this season and you'll get relegated."' County defied the criticism and finished second, resulting in promotion to the First Division. The boss had imposed a style of play on the training ground and the squad bought in to the philosophy.

At Wednesday, Wilkinson's style of football was far more direct than at Notts. This suited the players, most notably forward Lee Chapman, who thrived as the focal point in this system. 'Jack Charlton had been manager and there were centre-backs everywhere,' said Wilkinson. 'So I went with three at the back. We were one of the first in this country to do it.' It was another example of a manager breaking from the pack and wanting to be different from the rest. His Wednesday team won promotion in his first season in charge, finishing runners-up in 1983/84. The Owls stayed up in 1984/85, retaining their top-flight status, and continued to do so for the next three campaigns.

Wilkinson, though, believed that by working under financial constraints at Hillsborough, his team would eventually hit a glass ceiling. Talking to the *Yorkshire Post*, he said, 'I had an excellent relationship with [Owls chairman] Bert McGee. He was a gentleman, but at the end of my fifth season I had gone to the board and said, "Look, we have gone as far as we can go with some of these players and to bring about the change required to push us on will take money." I gave them a figure. The board, though, wouldn't budge. The club had been in deep trouble a few years earlier, nearly going to the wall. The board, all Wednesdayites, didn't want to ever be in that position again. I understood that.'

Fast forward to 1988 and Leeds were bang in trouble. The heady days of Don Revie were fast becoming a distant memory as the club was all but marooned in the second tier. Revie's Leeds were a dominant force during the 1960s and '70s, until he took the England job in 1974. Leeds had never even won a trophy until Revie brought success in the shape of the Second Division title (1963/64), two First Division championships (1968/69 and 1973/74), a League Cup (1968) and the FA Cup in 1972. This was all coupled with success in 1968 and 1971 in the Inter-Cities Fairs Cup.

Revie was a thorough man. He had dossiers on players, opposition managers and even referees. He was meticulous in his approach to games and was fiercely loyal to his players, with a squad including such class acts as Jack Charlton, Billy Bremner, Eddie Gray, Paul Reaney, Norman Hunter and Peter Lorimer. By 1988 these names were no longer around and Bremner had just been relieved of his duties after a poor run of results. Even so, the fans still adored their former captain despite his failed attempt at recreating the glory days. Leeds were favourites to gain promotion but could barely win a game and Bremner was handed his P45.

Chairman Leslie Silver wanted Wilkinson, but managing director Bill Fotherby played his part in the recruitment and had approached Bobby Robson. The then England manager met with Fotherby and politely turned down his advances. Fotherby, though, not to be disheartened, posed the question. 'I've been all over England, Italy and Spain. Who would you choose?' Robson knew exactly the man to suggest. 'There's only one man I'd go for,' said Robson. 'Howard Wilkinson.'

Rebuilding the club was going to come at a cost and Leeds were going to have to roll the dice in order to compete again at the very top. Wilkinson had been there with both Notts County and Sheffield Wednesday and knew exactly what was required to escape the Second Division but the question on his lips was how much the board was willing to spend to make the dream a reality.

In a meeting with Fotherby and Silver, it was estimated that around £2m–£3m would be needed to drag the club over the first hurdle, promotion. A further investment would then need to be made to ensure survival in the First Division. Wilkinson needed to be certain that the board were as ambitious as they claimed to be and not going to backtrack on any agreements regarding transfers. He had sailed that ship at Sheffield Wednesday.

The board were men of their word. Wilkinson walked through the doors at Elland Road and Gordon Strachan soon followed. The Scottish international from Manchester United was told by Alex Ferguson that his days at Old Trafford were numbered. 'He [Ferguson] turned up at my door at 7.30 in the morning to tell me that I would never play again for him,' said Strachan. The dynamic winger need not have worried though as his services were to be required across the Pennines in Leeds. As well as Strachan, Carl Shutt and Chris Fairclough were purchased, from Bristol City and Tottenham Hotspur respectively at just under £1m combined, beginning the rebuild.

Wilkinson reverted back to a flat back four. His sweeper system was left at Hillsborough and instead he opted for a more traditional formation. The new manager bounce was in full swing as Leeds managed a 0-0 draw at Swindon Town to stop the rot of four successive defeats. Two more draws followed as first Leicester City and then Bradford City provided stubborn opposition. Wilkinson was still getting to grips with his squad and in his fourth match in charge, he finally tasted victory with Ian Baird and John Sheridan scoring in a 2-1 win at home to Hull City.

Sheridan was something of an enigma who was adored by fans on the terraces but seemed to be at loggerheads with his manager. Under Bremner, Sheridan was given a bit of a free role both on and off the pitch. Wilkinson brought with him discipline and structure. The men soon gave him the nickname 'Sergeant Wilko' for his drill sergeant-style mannerisms on the training pitch. The team were drilled, and they were drilled hard. It was rumoured that on Wilkinson's first day, Sheridan never even bothered to turn up to training. Despite the lack of cohesion between the pair, Wilkinson knew that he had an ace in his pack who could pull the strings in the middle of the park. Consecutive wins followed with both Ipswich Town and West Bromwich Albion falling by the wayside.

Momentum in football is a wonderful thing and Wilkinson's side would not be beaten for 11 games, spread over two months, before eventually going down 3-2 at home to Shrewsbury Town. Leeds had clawed their way out the depths of the division and found themselves in a healthy mid-table position. They were also now beginning to see the demands placed on them by their new manager. Wilkinson's style was direct and coupled with hard graft. If players were not prepared to toe the line, then they were not going to be involved in the new revolution under Wilko.

The defeat to Shrewsbury was merely a blip as Leeds enjoyed a merry Christmas and happy new year. Three wins and two draws for the Whites meant that Wilkinson's men had again began to turn the corner into 1989. Unfortunately for Wilkinson, inconsistency in his team's performances during the second half of the season curtailed any realistic chances of promotion. Despite the upturn after his arrival in October 1988, Wilkinson soon realised that his squad lacked character and the fight to compete over a full campaign. Leeds had flirted with the top six before finally settling in tenth. It was not amazing, but the building blocks were in place for Wilkinson's first full season.

Fotherby was again approached to open the cheque book. The initial investment had been agreed, but now it was time to show exactly how much the board wanted to make it work. Wilkinson gave them a list of men who would be required to push the team on and take the club to the next level. It was going to be costly, but to what expense is success? Or failure for that matter. Five players were signed and each brought with them a raft of experience and ability. Wilkinson knew that bringing in such players would help aid the development of the youngsters, most notably David Batty and Gary Speed. Through the doors at the Fullerton Park training ground came Mel Sterland (Rangers), Mickey Thomas (Shrewsbury Town), John Hendrie (Newcastle United), Jim Beglin (Liverpool) and Vinnie Jones (Wimbledon).

Jones was signed and tasked with bringing not only some much-needed steel to the pitch but also inside a dressing room that Wilkinson thought lacked leaders. Fearing that he would get himself in hot water during his early period at the club, Jones got the full backing of his manager after an altercation between himself and two of his team-mates. When mocked about Wimbledon's long-ball style, Jones grabbed both men and offered to change their point of view by way of a good hiding in the car park. Wilkinson called Jones to his office and to the amazement of the player, told him in no certain terms that he was not in the wrong. 'That's exactly why I brought you here,' said Wilkinson. Strachan, on the other hand, relished the idea of playing alongside the fiery Jones. 'He's infectious in everything he does,' claimed Strachan. The Scottish winger had been handed the armband by Wilkinson as a sea of change swept over the club.

Not only had there been an influx of new playing staff on the pitch, off the pitch more changes were afoot. 'From the outside I saw Leeds as a city dominated by Don Revie,' Wilkinson told the *Yorkshire Post*. 'I told Leslie [Silver] at our first meeting that the person coming in had ghosts all over the place, which could not be ignored – and mustn't be ignored because they were great times. But now the party was over – and it had been for a while at Leeds. I took down all the old photos [from the Revie era] and said, 'When we are nearly as good as them then they can go back up.'

Leeds were once again seen as firm favourites for promotion as the beautiful summer sun shone down on St James' Park. Wilkinson and his men travelled to Newcastle to play a United side who themselves were heavily fancied for promotion in 1989/90. It would be a day to forget for Wilkinson and co as the Magpies ran riot with debutant Micky Quinn helping himself to four goals in a 5-2 rout. Bobby Davison and Ian Baird replied for the hapless Leeds who quite frankly played like strangers. *The Guardian* ran an article asking if Quinn's bow had been the greatest debut by any player to have played in this country. 'You are a fucking bargain, Mr Quinn!' shouted Newcastle boss Jim Smith. 'Now, go and get us promoted.' Smith later told the press that it was '*Roy of the Rovers* stuff'.

I would love to have been a fly on the wall in the boardroom that following Monday after the directors had backed the manager with all the players he wanted to win promotion, only to watch the team capitulate in front of their very eyes. Players will tell you that in football you always get a chance to right the wrongs as games come thick and fast. Tasting defeat on the opening day had hurt Wilkinson but the manager was made from stern stuff and when Middlesbrough came to town just a few days later, he saw it as an ideal opportunity to kick-start the campaign.

Vinnie Jones, who was the only new signing not to make an appearance at Newcastle, made his debut at Elland Road as a second-half substitute. Leeds almost instantly seemed to become more aggressive in style. A 2-1 victory, even by the way of an own goal for the winner, ensured that Wilkinson's men had earned their first three points of the season. There was a long way to go but they had at least made sure that the opening-day hiccup was quickly erased.

Three consecutive draws were followed by three wins as Blackburn Rovers, Stoke City and Ipswich Town all walked away with a share of the points whereas Hull City, Swindon Town and Oxford United were not quite as successful. The unbeaten run continued as teams were being swatted aside. Leeds travelled to Upton Park in the October to face a West Ham side who were desperate to upset the momentum that Wilkinson's team had created. The game was more blood than thunder with tackles flying in all over the pitch. The

Hammers had set up with a five-man defence but Leeds kept plugging away until a rare Jones strike sealed a hard-fought 1-0 win.

The London press were far from complimentary in their assessment of Wilkinson and his team, claiming that they were roughhousing their way through the division. 'The game was hard, as we knew it would be, but West Ham were the team who had three players booked, while we did not have anyone cautioned. The criticism we have received is totally unfair. It has astounded me,' said Wilkinson.

Chris Fairclough, at the heart of the defence, was starting to show why Wilkinson opted to bring him from the top tier. 'His was as good a defensive display as I have ever seen from anyone,' declared Gordon Strachan, who himself had played magnificently on the day. Jones had really established himself to the fans as a cult hero after his performance in this game. The support had been terrific with a reported 5,000 Leeds supporters cramming into Upton Park.

Following that victory, Leeds rolled out five wins in six matches before finally succumbing to defeat in mid-November for the first time since the opening weekend. Leicester City disrupted the run in a topsy-turvy match which finally ended 4-3 to the Foxes. Undeterred by the blip, Leeds would win their next game, 2-1 at home to Watford. Newcastle headed to Elland Road in the return fixture from game one and were also chasing a promotion place. Leeds, though, had revenge in mind and with the wounds from the thumping at the beginning of the campaign still weeping, they were in no mood for a repeat performance.

A solid 1-0 win brought confidence to the team, with Baird scoring the only goal and as the Christmas decorations went up, so did Leeds's league position. Wins over Middlesbrough and Brighton, both with clean sheets, meant that the Boxing Day clash at Sheffield United would be a yardstick of aspirations, with the Blades also vying for promotion. Dave Bassett's Blades were another team in fine form so the 2-2 draw was probably a fair reflection of both sides. Drawing away from home to your rivals is always considered a great result and nobody from Elland Road would have thought any different.

Wilkinson knew that his side had not achieved anything at the halfway point in the campaign, but as the 1980s rolled into the '90s, the boss had one last throw of the dice. Two players were added to the team to relieve some of the workload on an already-stretched squad as Lee Chapman and Chris Kamara joined from Sheffield Wednesday and Stoke City respectively. Chapman had worked with Wilkinson at Wednesday in the First Division and was a deadly target man whereas Kamara was brought in to act as cover with Batty, Jones, Strachan and Speed occupying the midfield roles.

LeedsLive described Chapman as 'like finally finding the WD40 and being able to turn the tap on' as well as being 'graceless but ruthless'. It didn't take him long to break into his stride with the forward netting eight times in ten matches as the Leeds bandwagon kept rolling on. Leeds would lose a game a month but they always followed up with wins to regain momentum. Victories over Oxford, West Ham, Sunderland and Portsmouth propelled them to the summit of the division in March 1990, until the final day of the month when Wolverhampton Wanderers halted the Wilkinson express at Molineux.

That defeat to Wolves brought a discombobulation to the side as the busy Easter period snagged up Wilkinson's men. No wins against Bradford City, Plymouth Argyle or Oldham Athletic meant that teams chasing could capitalise on the sudden loss of form. Wilkinson still had the utmost confidence in his men. His squad were still favourites in his eyes. Sheffield United smelt blood but their own nose was bloodied as they rocked up at Elland Road only to be packed back on their bus with their tails between their legs. Leeds found their feet again, and then some, with a 4-0 win over their promotion rivals.

Barnsley travelled to Elland Road with their own ambitions, albeit to stay in the division, but with their Yorkshire rivals sitting in 21st position, many believed that this was going to be the game that sealed promotion. Leeds went in front but managed to let slip two goals as Barnsley came from behind to gatecrash the party. Just days later, Leicester were in town and as Leeds had already had their fingers burnt at the hands of the Foxes earlier in the campaign, when Gary McAllister scored for the visitors, the home fans began to fear the worst. But in front of their biggest crowd of the season, Wilkinson's men fought hard to gain victory. Mel Sterland and Gordon Strachan scored to send the majority of the 32,597 punters home happy. Strachan's winner in the

84th minute was one of the sweetest-hit shots that you are ever likely to see.

Leeds had won promotion to the First Division. Wilkinson had achieved what was asked of him by Fotherby and Silver, whose backing had paid off. On the final day, Leeds needed to better or equal Sheffield United's result to win the title, having the comfort of a better goal difference. On a balmy day in May 1990, Leeds travelled to the south coast to play Bournemouth. The attendance on that final day was reported at over 9,000 but ask any Leeds fan, there were thousands more in the area. Outside the ground, on the beaches. You name it, they were there. And when Lee Chapman scored the only goal in the game, the hordes of supporters went wild. Leeds were champions.

With the First Division now entertaining Wilkinson and his men, the manager again approached the board for new players. Chris Whyte, John Lukic and Gary McAllister were brought in with Vinnie Jones, Ian Baird and Mickey Thomas heading the other way. Unfortunately for Jones, his solitary campaign with Leeds was due to both the emergence of Batty and the signing of McAllister, who had run the Whites ragged in the previous matches playing for Leicester. Lukic was a solid goalkeeper and a winner, who had starred for Arsenal in their dramatic First Division championship victory of 1989, while Whyte was brought in to partner the solid Fairclough at the heart of the defence. It appeared to be good business again by the astute Wilkinson.

After a decade of playing in the second tier, it was time for Leeds to assert themselves on the top division, just like they had done under Don Revie. The opening game at Everton proved that Leeds were not just there to make up the numbers as a 3-2 win was courtesy of goals from Fairclough, Speed and Imre Varadi. The first home match of the campaign was against fierce rivals Manchester United, for a real humdinger to re-introduce the Elland Road faithful to the big time. Alex Ferguson's men had won the FA Cup in 1990, an outcome that had pretty much saved Ferguson's job.

Policing issues meant that Leeds were unable to pack out Elland Road, although more than 29,000 supporters did manage to see the 0-0 draw. Four points from six meant Wilkinson's men were looking in great shape and it would evolve into a very successful season with not only consolidation, but a finishing position of fourth being achieved. Leeds did doubles over Everton, Chelsea and Derby, as well as going unbeaten against Manchester United and going down to the odd goal in nine at Liverpool in a 5-4 thriller.

Wilkinson's men had sparkled domestically with his talisman Chapman helping himself to over 30 goals in all competitions. For some it was a real eye-opener to see a team come from the Second Division and hold their own in such a manner. To the players and Wilkinson, it was just another day in the office. Sterland commented to the *Yorkshire Post*, 'The training was so repetitive. We would stay on the training pitch all day until we got it right.' This was mirrored by summer signing McAllister, who said, 'Howard was very diligent on practice, the muscle memory of things, the movements all became ingrained.'

Working hard time and time again on movement and patterns of play enabled the squad to have a grasp on awareness during games. They instinctively knew where each other would be. Opposition labelled Leeds as direct and route one, but this was not the case. A trademark sweeping move for Wilkinson's men would be a ball played out wide to Strachan, who would move inside, enabling space for Sterland to drive down the outside of the Scot, overlapping and receiving the ball in the right-hand channel before whipping over beautiful crosses into the box, which would be met by either the lethal Chapman, or the youthful Speed, arriving late at the far post.

This was not luck. It was hard work, knowing and trusting that your team-mates would do the correct things. Leeds took that ethic with them into the 1991/92 campaign. Jim Beglin, who had decided to retire due to niggling injuries, and Chris Kamara both left the club. Kamara had only been a bit-part player with the midfield four of Batty, McAllister, Strachan and Speed playing in the majority of games.

Wilkinson again got it spot on in the transfer market. Defenders Tony Dorigo and John Newsome were signed from Chelsea and Sheffield Wednesday respectively. At the other end of the pitch, the Wallace brothers from Southampton were also signed, with Ray and Rod swapping the south coast for Yorkshire. More important, though, was the signing of midfielder Steve Hodge from Nottingham Forest. Hodge, an England international, had a wealth of experience and with Kamara deciding his future lay elsewhere, Wilkinson needed further options in the central areas of midfield.

August 1991 saw Nottingham Forest and more notably, Brian Clough, as the opening game at Elland Road. Clough, who in 1974 had an ill-fated tenure at the club lasting a mere 44 days, was not exactly flavour of the month with the locals. Gary McAllister's goal ensured that he was sent packing with nothing more than a defeat. Clough's former midfielder Hodge then notched in the next match against Wilkinson's old club, Sheffield Wednesday, in a 1-1 draw. Two draws against Manchester United and champions Arsenal signalled that another eventful campaign was in the offing as Leeds would not lose a game until 1 October, with Crystal Palace denting an impressive start.

Over that period, Leeds were playing some scintillating football. Wins over Chelsea, Liverpool, Manchester City and Southampton set the foundations on which Wilkinson's side were building. They were fearless in their approach to games. Rivals Manchester United were also showing form and Ferguson's men had finished two places below Leeds in the previous campaign, with sixth spot not quite enough for them to emerge as title contenders. This time around, though, both teams were vying for the big prize.

They were attacking from the off and dismantling opponents at will. The particular beauty of this Leeds group was that they were now starting to share the goals around. The burden on Chapman was being shared by his team-mates with Strachan, Speed, Sterland, Hodge and McAllister all chipping in with vital goals. Following the defeat to Palace, Leeds fired four-goal salvos past first Sheffield United and then Notts County.

Momentum was again with the Yorkshire side as they registered seven wins in their next eight games, taking them into December in good nick. Unfortunately for Wilkinson, he was given the footballing equivalent of coal for Christmas as Leeds could not buy a win over the holiday period. Four games were played and all four ended in stalemate, including a 1-1 draw against Manchester United. Leeds would then play United again over a short period, this time in both domestic cups. United sent Leeds packing in both competitions, 3-1 and 1-0, although Wilkinson's men would ultimately have the last laugh.

With United navigating through those three matches unscathed, Ferguson's men became the favourites to claim a first title in 25 years. Wilkinson loved that. His team were now free to go about their business with the spotlight on the group from Old Trafford. As underdogs and now under the radar, Leeds were happy to let the rest take the limelight.

It was a happy new year for Wilkinson and co as first West Ham were beaten 3-1 in the capital and then they headed over to Sheffield to wallop Wednesday 6-1. Palace were in town but again proved to be an itch that Wilkinson could not scratch as a 1-1 draw halted the goal rush but even more concerning was the injury to Chapman, who had landed awkwardly on his arm. The first diagnosis was that the forward would be missing for eight weeks. With Wilkinson not wanting to lose any momentum, he looked to the loan market. Eric Cantona was signed from Nimes on an initial short-term deal which would be made permanent towards the end of the season. He had already pitched up in Yorkshire earlier in his career during a very short-lived trial stint at Sheffield Wednesday, so he was familiar with the area.

Chapman's absence was felt immediately as Leeds were held to a draw by Everton before tasting defeat at Oldham. Luckily for Wilkinson, however, Chapman was able to be patched up and brought back into the squad after missing just three matches. Strapped up and ready for action, Chapman scored on his return alongside his new partner Cantona, who also notched in a 2-0 win over Luton Town. Over at Old Trafford, Manchester United were relentless and were managing to rack up win after win.

Leeds then took Tottenham Hotspur apart 3-1 at White Hart Lane before a 5-1 demolition of Wimbledon at Elland Road. Chelsea were also victims of the steamroller as another three goals were scored to secure victory. April, though, would again see the crunch games come at a rapid rate of knots. United held a slender advantage at the top of the table but when they drew with Luton and then got turned over by Forest, Leeds pounced.

Liverpool were held 0-0 and then Coventry City were soundly beaten. United again stumbled at West Ham and with Leeds beating Sheffield United 3-2 in the penultimate game of the season, the Red Devils had to travel to Anfield to save their season. As a side-note, all five goals from Leeds's win over Sheffield United are of legend, so much so that there were even claims of match-fixing. I don't think anyone had ever seen a game where all five goals were so farcical. If you have never seen them, please use your favourite search engine and take a look. It will be the best five minutes of your day.

United had played four games in seven days and when Ferguson took his men to face Liverpool, needing a win to keep any title aspirations alive, weary legs and a hostile Kop combined to send them packing and deliver utopia for Leeds. United went down 2-0 and that was that. Wilkinson and his men were crowned champions of England, mirroring the feat twice achieved by the legendary Don Revie. 'Not all of those players would have been seen as the best in the world but they were committed to excellence,' said Wilkinson at the trophy presentation.

Licking his wounds at Old Trafford, Alex Ferguson said, 'Leeds United didn't win it, we lost it.' Sour grapes, maybe? There could be some truth in that, depending on which side of the Pennines you are from, but one thing is for sure, Wilkinson's Leeds were worthy champions. In three seasons the manager had won two titles and built a side that were to be the last top-flight winners managed by an Englishman.

The pictures of Revie were put back on the walls of Elland Road after the promotion season. Now Wilkinson was marching on together with some iconic imagery of his own.

11

Merseyside FC

A Decade Dominated by One City

Dominate
verb: have power and influence

LIVERPOOL IS a city of culture. The Beatles, Mel C, Ian Broudie and Cilla Black headline a list of singing sensations to hail from the city, not to mention Gerry and the Pacemakers. Actors Stephen Graham (*This is England*) and Ricky Tomlinson (*The Royle Family*) can also be traced back to this north-west hotbed of talent, and who can forget shows like *Brookside*, *Z-Cars* and *Bread*.

On the football spectrum, however, Liverpool have been a behemoth during the course of their history. Their most successful period was a 20-year stint through the 1970s and into the '80s. Big brothers Everton decided that they too would like a share of the pie, having watched their younger siblings receive trophy after trophy as first Bill Shankly led them to glory, followed by Bob Paisley, Joe Fagan and

Kenny Dalglish. It became a conveyor belt of trophies and as night follows day, for every managerial change the club made, the team just kept rolling on.

Not many eras had held a footballing rivalry like this one. Many cities have at least two teams, but with the exception of Glasgow, most are left to scrap for the right to be the big boy in town. London, for example, has sides in all different divisions but not many are in direct contact for honours. Milan hosts AC Milan and Inter. Both have had their share of honours but that has always been to the detriment of their rivals. While one team shares in the spoils, the other is left to admire from afar, casting a watchful but envious eye over its local counterpart.

To highlight my plight, Inter Milan have won the Italian title 18 times, the exact same amount as AC. Inter have finished runners-up on 15 occasions compared to AC's 17. In the Coppa Italia, Inter have seven titles compared to AC's five, with the teams finishing runners-up six and nine times respectively. That's a great haul between the two over a century of top-flight football but in all of those seasons of triumph, on only six occasions did the teams battle it out against each other. Inter won Serie A in 1964/65 and 1970/71 with AC finishing second. AC, however, edged out Inter in 1950/51, 1961/62 and 2010/11. The singular Coppa Italia Final meeting was a 2-0 victory for AC in 1977.

While I digress over two teams from northern Italy, the noticeable statistic here is that there was no prolonged assault by them both against each other. Juventus, Napoli and Roma often filled in the gaps left by whichever Milan side was not at the races. But over a ten-year period, the city of Liverpool was to witness both of its favourite sons going toe to toe on the canvas.

With the 1970s drawing to a close, Everton had to endure their neighbours lifting the First Division four times as well as one FA Cup, two UEFA Cups, three Charity Shields, a European Super Cup and back-to-back European Cups in 1977 and '78. In the same period, the Toffees could only muster a League Cup Final appearance and a third-place finish. The club nearly dropped out of the top tier for the first time in its history during the 1972/73 campaign, finishing 17th.

The famed 'Boot Room' at Anfield was where the coaches would gather to share their principles and ideologies. Bill Shankly had begun the assault on footballing domination at the tail of the 1950s. His reign lasted for 15 years before his right-hand man, Bob Paisley, took over in 1974. 'The only way to make the change over, is to promote the rest of the staff. They are sound and sensible men,' said Shankly, on his retirement.

Shankly had already set the tone for Paisley, who literally changed nothing. The Liverpool 4-4-2 steamroller just did not stop. Everton, meanwhile, were on their fourth manager of the decade in 1977 when Gordon Lee took the Goodison hotseat, taking over from caretaker manager Steve Burtenshaw. At first, Lee seemed to steady the ship with a third-place finish in 1977 but following on from that the Toffees slipped to 19th and 15th in 1980 and '81 respectively.

This signalled the end of Lee, who was replaced by Howard Kendall in May 1981. It was at this point that there was to be a sense of change in the city with Everton constantly having to watch on as those across Stanley Park succeeded time and time again. Liverpool had won the title in 1979/80 but their triumph was to be overshadowed as Nottingham Forest had claimed a second successive European Cup to shine even more light on Brian Clough at the City Ground, as if he needed any more.

The 1980/81 season for Liverpool had begun like many before that. Big wins and champagne football ensued but in an attempt to regain their status as Europe's elite, they took their eye off the ball in the league campaign. Only one defeat in their opening 19 matches, away to Leicester, painted a story of a strong start. Unfortunately for Liverpool, too many draws would curtail their assault on regaining their title as they would succumb to a fifth-place finish.

A replay was required to dispatch West Ham in the League Cup Final with Alan Hansen and Kenny Dalglish reversing an early lead from the Hammers. Everton, meanwhile, were languishing in the bottom half of the First Division despite only losing three of their opening 15 matches. A negative goal difference showed that there was more wrong than right on display at Goodison Park as the team again capitulated the longer the season wore on. A 15th-place finish was to be the final straw for the board and they made their move for Kendall, who was in charge at Blackburn Rovers.

Kendall had led Blackburn to fourth in the Second Division, narrowly missing out on promotion. The highlight, however, for the Toffees was the 2-1 win over

Liverpool in the fourth round of the FA Cup in January 1981. Despite being miles apart in terms of league positions and trophies won, in one-off games Everton would always fancy their chances.

The Reds had already demolished both Aberdeen and CSKA Sofia en route to the European Cup Final where they would meet another dominant force in Real Madrid, who at the time featured England winger Laurie Cunningham. Alan Kennedy notched the only goal in a narrow 1-0 win to add a third European Cup in six years to Paisley's collection. It was a quite remarkable achievement for the manager and of course his very talented squad, which featured the likes of Graeme Souness, Kenny Dalglish, Alan Kennedy, Ray Clemence, Phil Neal, Phil Thompson, Terry McDermott and Sammy Lee. Throw into the mix an up-and-coming striker by the name of Ian Rush and the Reds were looking in good shape.

Central defender Mark Lawrenson was signed from Brighton for a club record fee of £900,000 in the summer of 1981 to bolster an already impressive changing room. Howard Kendall also began a foray into the transfer market for Everton, bringing in goalkeeper Neville Southall from Bury. Southall was a young Welshman who was beginning to make a name for himself as an incredible shot-stopper. On entering Goodison for the first time, Kendall was approached by a waiting journalist. He was asked about his thoughts on his Everton squad, to which he replied, 'It's important to excite the fans. You need to put smiles on their faces when they leave the ground.'

There was most certainly an upturn in the results coming out of the blue side of the city despite Liverpool doing a league double over Everton with both matches ending 3-1. An eighth-place finish had brightened the gloom at Goodison, although they were clearly a work in progress. Kendall had instilled a strong work ethic among his players. Graeme Sharp notched 15 goals in all competitions for the Blues, while wonderkid Rush obliterated rival defences and doubled that amount with a haul of over 30.

Rush's goals had once again meant that Liverpool were the cream of English football, this time wrestling back their title from Aston Villa, who would coincidentally go on and take Liverpool's crown in the European Cup. Back-to-back League Cups were claimed as Tottenham Hotspur were taken to extra time and eventually beaten 3-1. The strength of this Liverpool team was that not only were they brilliant footballers, they also had some meat on the bones. Their team was full of real, hard men. They earned the right to play and once they did, they suffocated teams with a brand of football that just had teams waving the white flag. 'It's not about the long ball or the short ball,' Paisley once said. 'It's about the right ball.'

A blip in 1981/82 for Paisley and co. would have been the European Cup quarter-final exit to CSKA Sofia. Having led 1-0 after the Anfield fixture, complacency had clearly kicked in as Liverpool had beaten the Bulgarians soundly 6-1 on aggregate just a year earlier. What Paisley was not banking on was a very spirited performance from the home side and a 2-0 defeat in the second leg. It was back to the drawing board in Europe although with a First Division and League Cup double in the trophy room, another successful campaign had come to a close.

As the season kicked off in the warm August sun of 1982, Liverpool embarked on a bid to retain their title. Everton were also beginning to show promise. Brought in were Peter Reid, Derek Mountfield and Kevin Sheedy. Sheedy and Mountfield had not needed to relocate for the moves as they were signed from Liverpool and Tranmere respectively. They were local lads who knew exactly what the rivalry meant for both teams and their fans.

Nothing changed in the league as Everton were thrashed 5-0 at Goodison with Rush bagging four and Lawrenson wrapping up the scoring. The Toffees did, however, manage to salvage a draw and some pride at Anfield in the reverse fixture. Liverpool had only lost three matches by Easter and were champions again. A hat-trick of League Cups was also won as Manchester United were beaten 2-1 at Wembley. Paisley took a shine to the League Cup, which makes it all the more a shame that clubs nowadays use it as a throwaway competition. It is a great chance of not only silverware but a day out for all involved. Honours are forever, not just for Christmas.

The Blues would climb one spot to seventh but with Graeme Sharp again only scoring in the mid-teens, they did not have enough to threaten the top teams in the division. This was a sign of improvement but even so, when one of your siblings is constantly being treated for good work, it's a bitter pill to swallow when you have nothing to show for your efforts. No one wants to be a bridesmaid their entire life.

The bombshell on Merseyside was the retirement of Bob Paisley at the close of the 1982/83 season. 'This club has been my life; I'd go out and sweep the street and be proud to do it for Liverpool FC if they asked me to,' he said as he cleared his desk at Anfield. He went on to say, 'I've been here during the bad times too; one year we finished second.' Joe Fagan was installed as the new manager, again being promoted from within having been on the staff with both Shankly and Paisley.

Everton's 1983/84 campaign started slowly, to the point that there were whispers of the manager's job being in jeopardy. As the autumn grew into winter, Everton were languishing just above the relegation places and were not playing good football. There was just something missing. At this point, the only thing that Howard Kendall could put his finger on was that it was the crowd as just 13,659 punters turned up for Everton's home match against Coventry City in December 1983. Many of them were only there to voice their anger and not actually support the team.

On 18 January 1984, Kendall had one of those moments that could have turned the course of history against him. With Everton trailing Oxford United 1-0 in the quarter-final of the League Cup, Oxford's Kevin Brock sent a suicidal back-pass back to his goalkeeper with time ticking away at the end of the game. Adrian Heath reacted quickest and in a flash was on to the misjudged pass, rounded the hapless goalkeeper and rolled the ball into an empty net. Everton went on to win the replay 4-1 and kick-start Kendall's failing Goodison career.

Liverpool, despite losing back-to-back games in September, went on to lift their third First Division title in three years and a fourth in five seasons. Everton again finished seventh which was inconceivable after the form that they had shown up to the turn of the year. The consistency may not have always been there for Kendall but his players showed that in one-off games, they could be a match for anyone. Everton's change of fortune coincided with the start of their FA Cup campaign. Stoke City at their old Victoria Ground awaited the Blues and with Kendall feeling the pressure, he ensured that his team knew what was on the line. Goals from Andy Gray and Alan Irvine meant that Everton were in the hat for round four. This came just 11 days before that League Cup tie against Oxford.

Everton then marched to Wembley on two fronts. The semi-finals of the League Cup saw Liverpool and Everton avoid each other in the draw as the Blues faced Aston Villa whereas the Reds took on another Midlands side in Walsall. Both teams managed to get their respective jobs done, which meant that there would be an all-Merseyside final at Wembley for the first time.

With Everton attacking two competitions, their next task was to sidestep Notts County in the quarter-final of the FA Cup. This time a 2-1 victory proved enough for them to meet Southampton in the semi-final. The Saints were also chasing dreams of their own but when Heath scored with just three minutes of extra time remaining, it was too much for the coastal club to claw back and Everton were again in a final. Just a few short months previously, no one at Goodison could have anticipated that this would happen. All that was missing was a little belief. 'I knew what we were trying to build,' said Kendall. 'I looked around the training ground and just knew it would work.'

The League Cup Final in March 1984 was an all-Merseyside affair and Scousers flocked to the capital, some families even travelling together, although putting their colours first for just 90 minutes. The teams, however, had other ideas as neither could break the deadlock in a tense battle on Wembley's giant pitch as the two sets of 4-4-2 formations cancelled each other out. A 0-0 draw meant that they would have to do it again in a replay at Maine Road. Liverpool were in no mood to mess around this time as a single Souness strike was enough to claim the bragging rights and a record fourth League Cup in a row.

This didn't deflate Everton and instead it spurred them on. When Kendall and his men walked out again at Wembley just six weeks later, there was no way that anyone associated with the blue half of the city would want to feel that sinking feeling again. Goals from Gray and Sharp heralded Kendall's first trophy as Blues boss. Elton John's Watford were desperately unlucky, with Gray's second-half header being a very contentious talking point. 'Liverpool had better get used to sharing the spotlight on Merseyside from now on,' wrote Clive White for *The Times*.

Joe Fagan's inaugural campaign had ended with a treble of First Division, League Cup and European Cup. The Reds defeated Roma on penalties in a tense final, with Grobbelaar doing his famed jelly legs routine prior to one of the Italians' kicks during the shoot-out. Just when Everton thought that with Paisley leaving they might be in with a chance, along came Fagan to continue the work of his predecessors.

Between the two Merseyside clubs, they had cleaned up all before them. More importantly, for Kendall and his charges, there was to be a European assault in the shape of the Cup Winners' Cup to embark on. The new campaign had the Liverpudlians singing from the rooftops as both their teams had been worthy winners. But despite their cup success, the Toffees were desperate to close the gap in the bread and butter of the league and in 1984/85 they managed to turn the tables on their city rivals. First of all was another trip to the twin towers for the Charity Shield. They say charity begins at home and what more of a charitable way could Liverpool have presented the trophy to the Toffees. Alan Hansen, trying to clear his lines, cannoned the ball off the shins of Grobbelaar and into the empty net for a 1-0 Everton win.

But Everton's confidence was clearly knocked out of them on the opening day of the league season as a week later they were brought crashing back to earth with a thud. Tottenham went to Goodison and ran riot in a 4-1 thumping. Kendall reminded his team that this would need to be eradicated if they were to close the gap on Fagan's men.

A second defeat three days later, at West Bromwich Albion, shocked the team into a run of one defeat in 13 matches, including a 1-0 win away to Liverpool. It was to be the Christmas period that really got Everton in the mood. Winning 2-1 at Sunderland on Boxing Day sparked a run of 16 matches without tasting defeat. Liverpool were stuttering and an inability to turn draws into victories was proving to be a real sticking point for the Reds, who had lost Graeme Souness to Sampdoria in the summer.

Everton accumulated an incredible 50 points from 54 available as teams were simply blown away by the football and 4-4-2 system played by the Blues. Neville Southall was proving to be a solid base for the team to rely on. Gary Stevens and Pat Van Den Hauwe were marauding full-backs playing either side of Derek Mountfield and Kevin Ratcliffe. Kevin Sheedy and Trevor Steven provided the width while Peter Reid and Paul Bracewell had graft and guile. Leading the line were Graeme Sharp and Andy Gray. Adrian Heath had suffered a nasty injury and was unlucky to miss out on this carnival of football.

The only sour point in the season was the defeat to Grimsby Town in the League Cup. Kendall would be forgiven though as his cup runneth over with games coming thick and fast. The European campaign was also going well and having already dispatched University College Dublin, Inter Bratislava and Fortuna Sittard, the Blues were drawn against Bayern Munich in the semi-final of the European Cup Winners' Cup. After a goalless draw in Germany, Munich took the lead at Goodison. Everton rallied and goals from Gray, Steven and Sharp ensured that the Toffees would be heading to Rotterdam for the final.

The FA Cup was also in reach as Leeds United, Doncaster Rovers, Telford and Ipswich Town were put to the sword. Luton Town provided a sterner test and extra time was needed for Everton to continue their march back down to Wembley. Liverpool were hoping for a first all-Merseyside FA Cup Final but their hopes were dashed as they were beaten by Manchester United in the other semi.

Liverpool were also waving a white flag in the league and the gap was widening as Everton just kept on picking up points. The Reds were licking their wounds in the

League Cup as their quest for a fifth consecutive title was dealt a blow when Spurs beat them at White Hart Lane. Everton then clinched the title on 6 May with a 2-0 win at home to QPR and to make matters worse for Liverpool, the Toffees then turned them over a week later.

The blue half of Liverpool had put their noisy, younger sibling back into place and with the league in the bag, the Toffees headed to Holland to face Rapid Vienna. Everton were superb and blew away the Austrians in a 3-1 win to claim the first European title for the club. Gray, Steven and Sheedy scored to etch their names into club folklore.

The last throw of the dice for Fagan in terms of silverware was the European Cup. Liverpool had again reached the final and were looking at retaining the trophy, but they succumbed to a single goal scored by Juventus's Michel Platini as the Italians beat them 1-0. The game was overshadowed by the harrowing scenes of violence and crowd trouble as rival fans clashed before kick-off in the Heysel Stadium and a wall collapsed, killing 39 people and injuring many more.

The Liverpool fans were vilified for the incident and with the English supporters already having a bad reputation with the bigwigs at UEFA, the Reds were given sole blame. English teams were given a blanket and indefinite ban from all European competitions, effective immediately, which would ultimately be lifted in 1990, although Liverpool were not re-admitted until the following year. English clubs had dominated the European scene for nearly 15 years. To not have any representation was to be a real kick in the guts, more so for Everton, who would have their place in the European Cup cruelly taken away from them.

Everton, now running on empty, faced Manchester United in the FA Cup Final just a couple of days after their triumph in Rotterdam. The last thing Kendall and his men needed was a game on the big, energy-sapping Wembley pitch on a boiling hot day in May. The game was a slow, cagey affair and when United's Kevin Moran became the first man to be sent off in an FA Cup Final, it was looking nailed on that Everton would clinch a historic treble. United held on into extra time and with the run of games now starting to show in the legs of the Toffees, United capitalised with a superb goal from Norman Whiteside to clinch the game 1-0.

Liverpool had ended the 1984/85 season potless for the first time in over a decade. Joe Fagan resigned with many people fearing that the events at Heysel had taken their toll on the manager, who was deeply saddened by the events. Kenny Dalglish was appointed player-manager as again the Reds promoted from within. Across the city, Kendall moved to sign Leicester forward Gary Lineker, who was averaging a goal every other game, in order to keep the momentum going with his side.

Revenge was served to Ron Atkinson's team as United were soundly beaten 2-0 in the Charity Shield at Wembley. It was Everton's second victory in the fixture but then the league campaign got under way with an opening-day defeat to Leicester, which must have had Lineker wondering if he had made the correct decision in moving to Goodison. Liverpool began with a win at home to Arsenal and

Dalglish had thrown down the gauntlet to his men after a fruitless season.

Everton got back to winning ways and from then on traded blows with Liverpool each week. When one team won, the other followed. It was mesmerising stuff. Ian Rush was scoring goals for fun, as was Gary Lineker, who himself was playing as if the opposition didn't exist. With minimum midweek fixtures to prepare for, both sides were resting, working hard on the training ground and then dismantling their respective opponents on a Saturday.

To add to the drama, West Ham United were also in the mix for the title. It was tense. Everton were beaten by Oxford United at the end of April, opening the door for Liverpool and West Ham. Liverpool certainly didn't look the gift horse in the mouth and pounced, defeating Chelsea by a single Dalglish goal to take the trophy back across Stanley Park and into the Anfield cabinet. Everton clinched second by beating West Ham 3-1 to end any hope of a silver medal for the east Londoners.

A week after the league finale, on 10 May, Liverpool again faced Everton in a final for the second time in three years – this time the FA Cup was up for grabs. Liverpool lined up in a 4-4-2 formation but with Dalglish operating just behind the prolific Rush in a bit of a roaming role. Their side consisted of Grobbelaar, Nicol, Hansen, Lawrenson, Beglin, Johnston, Molby, MacDonald, Whelan, Dalglish and Rush. Everton were licking their wounds from the league humbling and when Lineker opened the scoring at Wembley, they sniffed blood. They couldn't hold on as Liverpool, with a half-time rollocking from their player-manager, came out a different side. Two goals from Rush and one from Craig Johnston proved the difference and brought a domestic double to Dalglish in his first season as boss.

Lineker, having opened the scoring, had notched his 40th goal in all competitions. It was a crying shame that this Everton team were unable to pit their wits in Europe as the enforced ban had been put into effect. Barcelona had reportedly been sniffing around the forward, albeit with Kendall denying any interest on several occasions. Critics would say that Lineker had taken his eye off the ball amidst the speculation as the title run-in became magnified.

In true football transfer fashion, only a matter of weeks into the summer Lineker was toasting a move to the Catalan capital. Liverpool, meanwhile, were about to lose a colossus of their own in the shape of Ian Rush. While Lineker was about to spread his English wings and head to Spain, Rush was also in need of reaching for his passport. Juventus had paid £3.2m, a record for a British player, for the services of the forward, who would be permitted to remain on loan for a season at Anfield.

With the double-winning Liverpool again facing Everton in the 1986/87 Charity Shield, it was a chance for the Toffees to end their recent hoodoo against the Reds. Adrian Heath looked to have won it late on for Everton until an equaliser by Rush with only four minutes remaining ensured that the honours were even.

Rush, determined to sign off with a flourish, scored another brace a week later as Liverpool began the defence of their title away at Newcastle United. Everton, missing their main goal threat, were now relying on other players to chip in. Heath's timely return to the squad was a shining light for the Blues who were looking to try and overturn Dalglish's side once more. The first derby of the season was held at Goodison Park and finished 0-0. Rush was still spraying in the goals but was unable to add to his early-season tally in this tense and tight affair. The reverse fixture was to be more fruitful for Rush as Liverpool brushed aside Everton in a 3-1 victory. The Welshman netted twice and former Everton man Steve McMahon also got himself on the scoresheet.

The goals were being shared around for Everton as they finished the campaign with winger Trevor Steven as their top league scorer with 14 goals. Steven, Heath and Sheedy all combined to net 48 times between them in all competitions, emphasising the teamwork showed by Kendall's charges. There was no player bigger than the team. It was a collective effort and would need to continue the whole way through if they were looking to hold off Liverpool as the season drew to its conclusion.

But Liverpool blinked first, and Everton finished 1986/87 with a second league title in three seasons. Rush had fired in 40 goals in all competitions but that tally was to no avail as Dalglish would finish trophyless. Liverpool also lost the League Cup Final after two strikes from Arsenal's Charlie Nicholas, despite taking an early lead through Rush. Dalglish knew that he had to replace Rush's goals if he was going to wrestle back the title from across Stanley Park. John Aldridge had been signed from Oxford United in the January of 1987 but was still finding his feet.

Forwards Peter Beardsley and John Barnes were also signed, from Newcastle United and Watford respectively.

Ray Houghton was brought in from the Oxford United side that had risen to prominence earlier in the decade. Having managed to grab a few words from Houghton when writing this book, I asked what it had been like to make the move to Liverpool at a time when it was a footballing city of both dominance and rivalry.

'They were rebuilding somewhat with Rush leaving so it was exciting times with the new players,' said Houghton. 'For sure the rivalry was intense and it was great for the city that both teams were doing so well. On arriving at the club I was told to just do my best, I'm sure it's the same for all the new players. There were no targets set, just take one game at a time. Don't get too much ahead of yourselves.' When asked about the omission from Europe, Houghton agreed, 'Yes, it was a shame.'

Neville Southall, Everton's world-class goalkeeper, echoed the sentiments of Houghton. 'Liverpool was buzzing. Great music and a great city full of genuine fans who were happy to see both competing to the max. Howard Kendall tried to win every game in every competition possible. We were the best team in Europe at the time.'

Another Charity Shield was added to the growing collection at Goodison Park with the 1987/88 campaign getting up and running with another Wembley win. Liverpool's season was also off to a good start with a 2-1 victory over Arsenal with Aldridge getting off the mark. A League Cup tie at Anfield then saw the two teams face each other, with Everton narrowly nicking a 1-0 smash-and-grab to go into the next round. It was revenge a week later as Beardsley and McMahon both grabbed goals to condemn Everton to defeat in a First Division fixture. The game at Goodison in the second half of the campaign was of little consolation for the Toffees as despite winning by a single goal, they had to settle for a fourth-place finish in the table.

Dalglish's men had again won the First Division and when they faced the very unfancied Wimbledon in the FA Cup Final, it was nailed on that they would achieve a second double in only three seasons. As we know from earlier chapters, this wasn't to be the case as the Crazy Gang upset all the odds to win courtesy of a Lawrie Sanchez header just eight minutes before half-time.

The beginning of the 1988/89 campaign saw the start of the new TV rights deal that ITV had struck. For the first time there was going to be live games, as well as a highlights package, exclusively beamed into homes all around the country. With this was now even more chance for viewers to see the best players in the First Division and witness first-hand the champagne football on display by some of the greats. Liverpool had re-signed Ian Rush from Juventus after just a solitary season on the continent. Everton, meanwhile, saw their mid-decade dominance begin to wane and they finished eighth in the table.

The ITV broadcasters, however, must have been rubbing their hands together as a one-game shoot-out between Liverpool and Arsenal at Anfield was to determine who would-be crowned champions. It was a Friday night and the final fixture of the campaign, delayed as a result of the Hillsborough disaster the month previously. Arsenal, needing to win by two clear goals, had a plan. Liverpool, attacking with intent from the off, realised that Arsenal were happy to soak up the pressure. This encouraged Liverpool themselves to then ease off the gas as it was the Gunners who needed victory, not the other way round.

When Alan Smith scored early in the second half, the sense of dread swept over Anfield. It's hard to pick yourself back up as a team once you have released your stranglehold over an opponent. With time ticking down, Liverpool were in possession. Barnes, with the ball at his feet and seemingly heading to the corner flag, then decided that he wanted to try and kill the game off. He cut inside only to lose possession.

How costly this proved to be, no one knew at the time. In the chain of events that followed, had just one link broken down then Liverpool would have retained their title. The ball fell into the hands of Gunners goalkeeper John Lukic. He threw it to full-back Lee Dixon, whose long pass into his forward Smith was flicked on towards the on-rushing Michael Thomas. The midfielder took what seemed an eternity to get the ball into his stride before prodding home past the hapless Grobbelaar.

Arsenal had clinched the title in arguably the most dramatic fashion of all time. While Sergio Agüero's goal for Manchester City in the 94th minute of the final day to win them the 2012 Premier League title was thrilling, at the expense of their city rivals, but not more so than the actual two teams who were going at it hammer and tongs.

Had Barnes headed into the corner instead of trying to make something happen, Liverpool could well have closed the game out. It proved to be a sliding doors moment as just a minute or so later, their grip on the trophy had all but been relinquished.

Liverpool had finished as runners-up to George Graham's Arsenal and missed out on the double, having won the FA Cup a few days previously.

Before 1984, there had never been an all-Merseyside final in either of the two cup competitions. That first League Cup Final had been followed two years later by an FA Cup Final, then the world's oldest cup competition once again saw the two teams meet in the showpiece in 1989.

The final weeks of the 1988/89 season had been overshadowed by the harrowing events at the semi-final between Liverpool and Nottingham Forest at Hillsborough, and what would prove to be the biggest sporting tragedy on English soil as 96 Reds supporters lost their lives following crushing and overcrowding on the Leppings Lane terrace. When the match was eventually replayed, Liverpool were victorious and waiting for them at Wembley were, fittingly, their Merseyside rivals. Everton lined up for the final with Southall, McDonald, Van Den Hauwe, Ratcliffe, Watson, Steven, Nevin, Bracewell, Sheedy, Sharp and Cottee. Liverpool went with Grobbelaar, Ablett, Staunton, Nicol, Hansen, Houghton, Barnes, Whelan, McMahon, Beardsley and Aldridge.

Ian Rush was left on the substitutes' bench by Dalglish, which was a talking point in the stands prior to kick-off as 82,000 Scousers crammed into Wembley to witness what was to be an absolute humdinger of a tie. Liverpool took the lead in the fourth minute with their first attack of the game. In the hot May sun, Steve McMahon broke clear of the Toffees back line. Looking up, McMahon squared the ball to Aldridge who side-footed home with aplomb. There were huge sighs of relief from the Irishman, who had missed a penalty in the Reds' final defeat to Wimbledon a year previously.

As the seconds ticked down towards full time, Everton streamed players forward in a bid to equalise. A goalmouth scramble saw Grobbelaar clear his lines as Liverpool began to get tetchy. Then with the game all but finished, a final Everton attack down the right landed to Steven whose cross was not dealt with by the Liverpool back line. Stuart McCall threw himself into the melee and managed to toe-poke the ball into an empty net, taking the final to extra time.

Rush, a second-half replacement for Aldridge, received the ball on the penalty spot with his back to goal after five minutes of the additional half-hour. In the blink of an eye, Rush spun his marker and fired the ball into the far corner of the net to put his team 2-1 up. Kevin Ratcliffe, the man turned by Rush, atoned seven minutes later. A free kick by the defender was angled into the Liverpool penalty area where the Reds cleared their lines, only for the ball to drop to McCall who was waiting patiently just outside the penalty box. The substitute chested down and fired a sweet volley into the bottom corner of Grobbelaar's goal for 2-2.

But, just as night follows day, Rush struck again for his second of the game, repeating his feat from the 1986 final. Barnes, picking up the ball just outside of the Everton area, delivered a sublime left-footed cross into the box. Rush, unmarked, stooped low to angle a header past the flat-footed Southall who could only watch as the ball trickled into the corner. Liverpool managed to hold on to clinch another FA Cup at the expense of their city rivals. The win, and more importantly the performance from both sides, lifted the spirits of the supporters after a turbulent few weeks after Hillsborough.

The 1980s belonged to the city of Liverpool. Both sets of fans had witnessed success, as well as the lows that come with defeats, and by the end of the decade they had been brought closer together than ever following the events at Hillsborough. 'We were not only great individual players, but played as a team,' said Howard Kendall. The team that Howard built had managed, for a short time, to go toe to toe with Liverpool. Blues fans will never forget that. Kendall will forever be revered by the blue half of Merseyside as the man who gave them the bragging rights, and the chance to walk the streets with their heads held aloft. But let us not forget the impeccable work carried out by Bob Paisley, Joe Fagan and Kenny Dalglish. For the neutrals, what great viewing both teams gave us all.

12

Kipling and Barclay

PATRICK BARCLAY has spent a large portion of his life covering some of the finest teams to have ever graced the field. Barclay had worked at *The Guardian*, *Independent*, *Sunday Telegraph*, *Observer* and *The Times*, where he became its chief football correspondent. Besides the day job, several biographies were penned as well as appearing on shows such as *Sunday Supplement* on Sky Sports and *Scores* on the radio station LBC. His books include works on both Sir Matt Busby and Sir Alex Ferguson, as well as José Mourinho and Herbert Chapman.

Sometimes in life you get an opportunity to chat with people who have seen such greatness with their own eyes. This was one of those times, so here is a transcript of our conversation. Patrick's comments are in bold.

I see that having done my homework, you were covering football around the time when Brian Clough was in charge at Derby County and Nottingham Forest? **'Yes,** particularly the Nottingham Forest era. I remember that when I first came into it, one of the first people that I tried to interview was Clough and he said, "You can come down for a game of squash but you're not getting a fucking interview."'

He's brilliant, isn't he? 'Clough said, "If you did play then you might get a couple of words with me." I remember the great Juventus team with [Didier] Deschamps and [Zinedine] Zidane playing in a diamond as the midfield. I said to Howard Wilkinson at the time, is that the perfect midfield combination of Deschamps' pragmatism and Zidane's fantasy? As always with Howard he would never give an easy answer and he said "yes and no, no being that if you could saw them in half, you would have two who could do everything". And I have thought about that a lot since. He was a bit ahead of his time there.

'I still yearn for the two strikers. I think it's more difficult for a defender to defend against two than against a three. It's very rare that one of the wide men in the three, come inside to join the striker.'

I agree, they tend to stay quite high and wide, like wingers who turn into inside-forwards rather than playing inside the width of the 18-yard box. 'Of course. Nobody scores a goal from the touchline.' With only one forward to worry about and three midfielders sat in front of the defenders, there is not as much concern about being turned as the lone forward will more than likely always want the ball to him and not in behind. 'Four-four-two in this country was always our bread and butter. It got us a bit of a bad reputation because of the England team becoming such an underachiever.' Yes, I think that the tipping point was that the final nail in the coffin was hammered in after the performances during the 2010 World Cup finals, particularly against Germany. I believe that it was a transition period with the end of the 'Golden Generation'. 'Correct.' We looked very slow and lethargic.

If we are talking 4-4-2, big man-little man and wingers, which team in your journalism career would you say you enjoyed covering the most? 'A lot of the Manchester United performances, especially the 1999 treble-winning team, and the year before and the year after, you know with Yorke and Cole, who to me were fantastic. You couldn't get a better pair of different wingers, with all due respect to Steve Coppell and Gordon Hill, than David Beckham and Ryan Giggs. Totally different players but stretching the opposition to death. And then you have Roy Keane and Nicky Butt winning the ball in midfield, with the passing of Paul Scholes. I mean that team would have to be up there. But another team which comes to mind is the Everton team of the mid-'80s. We will never know how good that team will have ever been because it had the guts kicked out of it by the exclusion of European football after the Heysel disaster. They had won the European Cup Winners' Cup with something verging on ease, although they did have one tough tie in Bayern Munich in the semi-finals. The team of 1987 that won the league title was nowhere near as good as the 1985 side.

'The Leeds United team that won the last First Division title under Howard Wilkinson, they had as good a middle four as you would want to see. For balance in a midfield, you want a playmaker? Gordon Strachan. You want a quality passer, try Gary McAllister for size. You want a ball winner? David Batty. With all of that, where's the height? Try Gary Speed. Fantastic in the air. That four was perfect for balance. If you were comparing them to the treble side of Manchester United, then they would come up slightly short.'

Leicester City played with that 4-4-2 formation. Why do you think they were so successful, culminating in them winning a fairytale title, when everyone else was still playing in a 4-3-3 or 4-2-3-1? 'I think it came from Claudio Ranieri being clever enough to look at the team and say right, my job here is to get the best out of Jamie Vardy because this guy is a phenomenon. He stuck the incredibly hard working Okazaki in behind Vardy and gave Vardy space. I say behind, they played as two strikers but they didn't interchange as much. You wouldn't see Vardy dropping short for Okazaki to spin in behind. It wouldn't have made any sense. It was predictable, except no one could stop it. Mahrez was a magician. He ended up becoming the second top scorer in the team, scoring more than Okazaki. You also had the long passing of Danny Drinkwater. I wouldn't say that Okazaki was the best player in the team, but he was the most underrated contributor out of those 11.'

We touched on it earlier with the introduction of foreign coaches bringing over new ideas, but do you think that they have ruined the English tradition? Or do you think that they have in fact elevated the tactical styles that we now see? 'It's a good question. Did it accelerate the process with the introduction of José Mourinho? Or the longevity of Arsène Wenger? Probably. Mourinho made the 4-3-3 or 4-5-1 popular as when he arrived at Chelsea, he blew away the league for two seasons running. He switched from his 4-4-2 diamond that he played at Porto as the players he had at his disposal at Stamford Bridge were more suited to a more expansive style. He was clever enough to see that and it worked magnificently for him. The English 4-4-2 formation was never really the same after that.'

Do you think that 4-4-2 will ever come back into fashion? 'Yes! I do because I think that most things do come back into fashion, particularly things that have proved that they are successful. There are a couple of instances of it recently where people are starting to toy with the two strikers again, because as mentioned before, it's difficult for defenders. After all, it wasn't something that was shown to be ineffective, it wasn't something that English clubs laboured under. Okay, the national team may have underachieved during the time of the golden generation but maybe that was partly because the two central midfielders, Steven Gerrard and Frank Lampard, as mentioned by Joey Barton, "needed a ball each". I thought he produced a brilliant phrase on that occasion.'

On the silver screen, the 4-4-2 formation was highlighted in the satirical comedy *Mike Bassett: England Manager*, starring Ricky Tomlinson in the lead role. Having staggered through the World Cup finals, Bassett was expected to announce his decision to step down from his position during a press conference. A draw against unfancied Egypt and a mauling at the hands of Mexico left England and Bassett in hot water. A final group game against old foe Argentina awaited and England needed to win to stand any chance of progressing into the final stages.

Having bowed to media pressure and with the advancements of modern football, Bassett had trialled several formations, without success. A drunken bar brawl with his assistant was not going to help matters and with emotions running high, Bassett addressed the waiting world in poetic style:

'If you can keep your head when all about you are losing theirs and blaming it on you; if you can trust yourself when all men doubt you, but make allowance for their doubting too; if you can wait and not be tired by waiting, or being lied about, don't deal in lies, or being hated, don't give way to hating, and yet don't look too good, nor talk too wise.

'If you can dream – and not make dreams your master; if you can think – and not make thoughts your aim; if you can meet with triumph and disaster and treat those two impostors just the same; if you can bear to hear the truth you've spoken twisted by knaves to make a trap for fools, or watch the things you gave your life to, broken, and stoop and build 'em up with worn-out tools.

'If you can make one heap of all your winnings and risk it on one turn of pitch-and-toss, and lose, and start again at your beginnings and never breathe a word about your loss; if you can force your heart and nerve and sinew to serve your turn long after they are gone, and so hold on when there is nothing in you except the will which says to them, "Hold on!"

'If you can talk with crowds and keep your virtue, or walk with Kings – nor lose the common touch, if neither foes nor loving friends can hurt you, if all men count with you, but none too much; if you can fill the unforgiving minute with 60 seconds' worth of distance run, yours is the Earth and everything that's in it, and – which is more – you'll be a man, my son!

'Ladies and gentlemen, England will be playing four-four-fucking-two.'

'4-4-2 in this country was always our bread and butter. It got us a bit of a bad reputation because of the England team becoming such an underachiever.'

Patrick Barclay, Football Writer

An Ode to Four Four Two: Football's Simplest and Finest Formation, examines how coaches in Europe, and particularly England, settled on the 4-4-2 system to build iconic teams that would dominate, both domestically and in Europe.

Since the birth of the game in the mid-19th century, football formations have continually evolved – from teams playing with four or five forwards, to the modern era of teams fielding just one. But arguably the greatest formation is the classic 4-4-2. Some of the world's best sides have lined up in this multi-functional system.

Flick through the football history books and they are filled with teams enjoying glorious eras playing 4-4-2 – from AC Milan and Barcelona to Manchester United, Liverpool and Leeds United. But it isn't just the elite who've used the system to brilliant effect. Remember when 5,000-1 underdogs Leicester City captured an historic Premier League title in 2016, after club coach Claudio Ranieri revived the 4-4-2 system?

The book delves deep into the football annals to tell the compelling tale of how teams, both big and small, have played the system to perfection.

 Pitch Publishing @pitchpublishing

 Tweet about this book to @pitchpublishing using #AnOdetoFourFourTwo

Read and leave your own book reviews, get exclusive news and enter competitions for prize giveaways by following us on Twitter and visiting www.pitchpublishing.co.uk

9 781785 318382 >

Football   RRP: £12.99